KU-487-087

(25)

The Life and Times of
EDWARD VII

OVERLEAF, LEFT The coronation of Edward VII
in 1902, from the painting by S. Amato.
The King is depicted surrounded by the
various regiments of the British Empire.
RIGHT The Imperial State Crown, which
contains part of the Cullinan diamond,
presented to Edward VII by the Boers in
1907. When mined, it was the largest
diamond in the world.

The Life and Times of
EDWARD VII

Keith Middlemas

Introduction by Antonia Fraser

Book Club Associates, London

© George Weidenfeld
and Nicolson Limited
and Book Club
Associates 1972

First published 1972
Reprinted 1972

*All rights reserved. No part
of this publication may be
reproduced, stored in a
retrieval system, or
transmitted, in any form
or by any means electronic,
photocopying, recording or
otherwise, without the prior
permission of the copyright
owner.*

*Designed by Juanita Grout
Filmset by Keyspools Ltd,
Golborne, Lancashire
Printed and bound in Great Britain by
Morrison & Gibb Ltd, London & Edinburgh*

Contents

Introduction

A WARMTH OF POPULAR FEELING surrounds the royal image of King Edward VII – seen as the *bonhomous* and stately embodiment of the age to which he gave his name. As long as we continue to invest the Edwardian era with a reputation for delicious if somewhat upholstered pleasures, the personality of King Edward himself will surely continue to arouse the same nostalgia. In fact this superficial warmth was also a feature of King Edward's own brief (nine-year) reign, or as George Dangerfield cynically expressed it in *The Strange Death of Liberal England*: 'He represented in a concentrated shape those bourgeois kings whose florid forms and rather dubious escapades were all the industrialised world had left of an ancient divinity.' It was hardly surprising that in 1909 when the King's horse won the Derby – a royal record – the crowd roared 'Good old Teddy' and sang 'God Save the King'. Equally characteristic of the people's mood was the jingle of the same period which christened Edward 'The monarch to make things hum, The King, the runabout King'.

But popular images can be misleading and not every adventure of the 'runabout King' involved a rendezvous with a professional beauty at a foreign watering-place, or a high society scandal such as the Mordaunt divorce or the Tranby Croft baccarat case. For one thing, whatever the irony of it in view of his own behaviour, King Edward was the centre of a happy family life, had tender relations with his children (certainly more successful in this respect than his own mother Queen Victoria in her attitude to him as Prince of Wales) and retained the complete devotion of his wife Alexandra. More relevant still to a proper knowledge of the King's life is the vital position his reign occupied in the development of the constitutional position of the monarch – the King's advisers, Knollys and Esher, and his Prime Ministers, including Balfour and Asquith, being more central if less glamorous figures in its unfolding than Mrs Keppel and Lillie Langtry. The truth was by no means clear – a problem amply shown up by the great crisis over the passage of the Finance Bill by the House of Lords, still unresolved at the time of King Edward's death in 1910. Queen Victoria had certainly interpreted her right to offer advice to her ministers freely, while Edward's son George V held a position which was much nearer to that of the purely constitutional monarch as we understand it today. Keith Middlemas traces brilliantly the political map of the reign, delineating precisely those areas, such as army reform and the growth of the navy, where the King did actively interfere in affairs of state, and estimating how much practical effect, if any, resulted from these exercises of the royal will.

There was a third possible area of the King's influence – the highly complicated sphere of foreign policy in the years before the 1914 War – where once again a popular notion, that of 'Edward the Peacemaker', holds sway in the historical imagination. Was King Edward in fact the architect of the Anglo-French *entente cordiale*, or did his personal taste for travel and Parisian life in its gayer forms merely coincide happily with a period when British foreign policy was already moving away from 'splendid isolation' towards the embrace of Europe? Here once again Keith Middlemas disentangles myth from reality with admirable lucidity. The result is a remarkable double portrait, showing both the man and the monarch, certainly a much fuller and more interesting composition than the conventional portly *roué* of folk memory.

Antonia Fraser

Acknowledgments

Photographs and illustrations were supplied by and are reproduced by kind permission of the following:
The photographs on pages *14-15*, 18, 22/2, 23, 28, 36, *62-3*, 90/1 are reproduced by gracious permission of H.M. the Queen. Bassano & Vandyk: 106/2; B.P.C: 170, *180/2*; Art Institute of Chicago: 193/1; Conservative Research Department: *180/1*; A.C.Cooper: 22/3, 23, 36; Mary Evans Picture Library: 85, *177*; John Fleming: *50-1*; John Freeman & Co.: 22/1, 61, 77/1, *109*, 159; Gernsheim Collection, University of Texas, Austin: 10-11, 30, 44, 75/2, 89, 90/2, 102-3, 107, 111; Giraudon: 13/1, 13/2, *192/2*; William Gordon Davis: 19, 84/2, 95, 127, 129, 136, 152-3, 184-5; Guildhall Art Gallery: *50-1*; Heinemann: 49; Henry Huntington Library, California: 122-3; London Museum: *112/1, 112/2*, 193/2, 198, 199; Longman, Green & Co.: 24; Mander & Mitchenson Theatre Collection: *192/1, 192/3*; Mansell Collection: 29/1, 29/2, 54, 55, 64, 141, 148, 163, 175, 182-3, 191, 201; Jonathan Martin: 187/2; Metal Box Company Limited: 118/3; Ministry of Public Works (Crown Copyright): *3*; Montagu Motor Museum: 190-1/2; Moro, Rome: *2*; National Portrait Gallery: 48/1, 48/2, 84/1, *97, 100*, 126-7, *189*, 203; Mrs Norbury: *109*; Oxford Public Libraries: 70-1/3; Popperfoto: 118/1, 119, 162, 216-7; Radio Times Hulton Picture Library: 17, 25, 27/1, 27/2, 28, 32, 35, 37/1, 42/2, 66-7, 74, 77/2, 78, 84/3, 91/1, 91/2, 94, 99, 120, 131, 137, 143/1, 143/2, 186-7/1, 190-1/1, 208-9, 210, 213; George Rainbird Ltd: *109*; Royal Academy: 18; H. Tasiemka: 165, 174; Tate Gallery: 70-1/1, 200; Todd-White: 24, 112/2; Château of Versailles: 13/1, 13/2; Victoria and Albert Museum: 37/2, 49, 75/1, 196/3; Derrick Witty: 196/3.

The author owes acknowledgment to the following for quotations: Philip Magnus, *King Edward VII*, John Murray (Publishers) Ltd (1964): Sir Frederick Ponsonby, *Recollections of Three Reigns*, Eyre and Spottiswoode (Publishers) Ltd (1951): George Dangerfield, *The Strange Death of Liberal England*, Constable, London (1936): *The Dictionary of National Biography* (2nd supplement, 1912), introduction by Sir Sidney Lee, by permission of the Clarendon Press, Oxford: *Memories*, volume 1 of *Some Recollections* by Lord Fisher (London: Hodder and Stoughton, 1919), used by permission of the publishers: Harold Nicolson, *George V*, Constable, London (1952): quotations from *The Times* are reproduced by permission.

1 A Victorian Upbringing 1841-61

'A WONDERFULLY STRONG and large child with very large dark blue eyes, a finely formed but somewhat large nose and a pretty little mouth.' So Queen Victoria described her first son to her uncle, King Leopold of Belgium. He was born, she added, after 'very severe' suffering on the morning of 9 November 1841, four years after she herself had come to the throne at the age of eighteen. The birth was the second within a year, Victoria having already produced a daughter, Vicky, in the previous November.

The omens which surround the birth of princes were on this occasion somewhat trivial. Since the future Edward VII arrived at 10.48 a.m. and the guard at St James's Palace changed at 10.45, a dispute arose as to which officer in command was due for promotion. As heir to the throne, the baby became at once Earl of Chester and the current mayor was therefore entitled to a baronetcy, but the office changed hands on 9 November at no specified hour. No minor questions of court etiquette, however, could offset the triumphal fact that for the first time since 1762, in the reign of George III, a male heir had been born to the House of Hanover during the reign of the sovereign – ample cause for celebration for the family and for the dynasty of which it was part.

As far as Victoria was concerned, her son was intended to be a replica of the virtues of her husband, Prince Albert. Married in February 1840 to this scion of the Saxe-Coburg-Gotha line, Victoria had fallen deeply in love with the handsome, intellectual Prince and had totally merged her character in his. 'He seems perfection, I love him more than I can say,' she wrote before their marriage; while Albert commented more soberly, 'I think I shall be very happy'. True, Albert's family background was not unsullied – his mother had been divorced by Duke Ernest (himself no paragon of virtue) in 1826 and there was a rumour that Albert was the product of a liaison between the Duchess and Baron von Meyern, a court chamberlain of Jewish extraction – but then the House of Hanover had a record that was of dubious credit. To the insanity of George III was added the loose-living of George IV, and neither he nor William IV had added much lustre to the monarchy during the previous twenty years. However, Victoria's youth and innocence helped to usher in a period of respectability, and she adopted her

PREVIOUS PAGES In the Royal Nursery: a sketch by John Doyle showing Queen Victoria and Prince Albert with their eldest children. The Prince of Wales is playing the harp.

husband's seriousness and dedication as a model for herself.

In the wake of the 1832 Reform Act and the increasing involvement in politics of the wealthier section of the middle class, the monarchy was already seen as a position of trust, embodying the twin duties of setting a moral example to the Queen's subjects and of serious application to the tasks of government. Although Albert's solemn manner and lack of humour made an unfavourable impression on the public – to judge by the hostile cartoons which appeared after the marriage – his naturally studious nature was well fitted to the task of creating a style suitable to a powerful industrial nation, which had in many ways outgrown the laxity of the Regency. The relationship between the Queen and Albert conformed to the middle-class paradigm of devotion and mutual affection and it was undoubtedly the most formative influence in Victoria's life, shaping, above all, her attitude towards her children. Lord Melbourne, her Prime Minister, objected to the names Albert

Prince Albert and Queen Victoria, as painted by Winterhalter in 1842, the year after Edward was born.

OVERLEAF The Imperial Hunt in the Forest of St Germain, 25 August 1855. This painting by Hippolyte Bellange shows the visit of the Prince of Wales, Prince Albert, Queen Victoria and Princess Royal to Napoleon III of France.

13

Edward – he preferred 'a good English appellation' – but all the royal children had Albert included among their names, if boys, and Victoria if they were girls. Of the first-born son, Victoria's own hope was 'to see him resemble his angelic dearest father in every respect, both in body and mind'.

In dynastic terms, the birth added another wreath to the House of Saxe-Coburg which, though only minor German royalty, had succeeded to the throne of Belgium and married into many of the royal houses of Europe in the years following the Napoleonic Wars. Although the personal union of the crowns of the United Kingdom and Hanover had ended with William IV, the British monarch was still tied to Europe by important dynastic ties. Because of the connections of the British royal family Victoria was sometimes called 'the Mother of Europe', and by the time he succeeded to the throne in 1901 Edward could lay claim to the title of 'Uncle of Europe'. He was born seven years before the monarchic system on the Continent underwent the shock of the revolutions in 1848 and even these, while subtly changing the rules of the diplomatic game, had little effect on the personnel of the players. Until 1914 monarchs still influenced the lives of millions through their conduct of foreign policy. The universal rejoicing in Britain may have reflected, at a popular level, not only acceptance of the stereotype of monarchy as supreme characteristic of the national interest, but also a shrewd appreciation that a native male heir would counter-balance the Germanic tradition at court.

The power and influence of the sovereign was, in theory, by no means so restricted as it became later in the reign, when Bagehot could enunciate his famous principle that the role of the wise monarch should be confined to 'the right to be consulted, the right to encourage, the right to warn'. In the 1840s the monarch's degree of control of government policy was still technically unrestricted. Victoria herself had at first chafed at the position of a strictly constitutional monarch, which involved bending her will to the demands of different sets of party politicians. If Albert had a more rigidly constitutional conception of the monarch's relation to political parties, this did not preclude an active part in the process of decision-making. Albert and his closest adviser, Baron Stockmar, had clear views on British

16

foreign policy – not unconnected with their desire to see Germany united. The Prince Consort maintained so insidious a part in the running of the administration that Lord John Russell could speak of him as 'an informal but potent member of all Cabinets'. Lord Clarendon acknowledged the Prince's intimate knowledge of the workings of all government departments. The more sober monarchy which Albert sought to institute, far from precluding a positive role in government, encouraged just such a trend. The powers of the sovereign were exercised less openly than on the Continent, a factor that was to lessen the resentment which boiled over in 1848 against arbitrary personal power in government and which left the British monarchy in a relatively stable position thereafter. But the sovereign was a permanent part of the executive. Victoria could exercise a constant influence, especially in the conditions of mid-nineteenth-century politics, when the parties were often evenly balanced, and she felt quite free to seek to impose her views on the appointment of ministers and the conduct of policies.

Baron Stockmar, Prince Albert's close friend and counsellor, who was partly responsible for the scheme drawn up for Edward's education. His stern disciplinary views were to have a disastrous effect upon Edward's youth.

Thus Albert Edward was heir to a position of power and influence notably secure in comparison with that of his European relations. From the first moments of his life, his status was embodied in the royal formalities. On 4 December he was created Prince of Wales by patent under the Great Seal, and on 25 January 1842 he was baptised in St George's Chapel, Windsor, by the Archbishop of Canterbury. The ceremony was suitably impressive – some £200,000 were spent on the occasion, and a christening cake eight feet across was produced. His godfather was Frederick William IV of Prussia, who bestowed on him the Order of the Black Eagle as a christening present.

Then, after the trumpets and the glory, came the protracted education of the child. The Prince passed to the royal nurseries, into the care of Lady Lyttleton, a daughter of Lord Spencer. She was, perhaps, the gentlest of his tutors. One biographer referred to her 'maternal tenderness mingled with common sense', and from her the Prince got his grounding in languages. German, at least, was no problem. So strong was the influence of German at court that Edward picked it up more quickly than English and to the end of his life tended, even in public, to introduce the gutteral German 'r'.

The christening of Edward at St George's Chapel, Windsor, 25 January 1842, as painted by Hayter.

OPPOSITE Winterhalter's painting of Edward as a child.

The first seven years of Edward's life were the most relaxed, the only ones of his youth in which he was free from the rigorous disciplines of schooling which characterised his up-bringing. The education of a future ruler proved to be a matter of high concern. Just as Plato had laid down the principles for schooling the rulers of the Republic, so the most eminent minds were called in to advise here. Gladstone and Macaulay, the historian, spoke with awe of Edward's future destiny. Others reflected uneasily on the past, on the abhorred memory of George IV, embodiment of everything Albert and Victoria detested. Lord Granville set the cat among the pigeons with a reference to Edward's 'incipient propensity to that sort of romancing which distinguished his Uncle' – and the halcyon years were over. Advice on future discipline came from many quarters, all indicating that a 'serious' training would produce what Bishop Wilberforce aptly defined as 'the most perfect man'. Only Lord Melbourne, sensibly humane, warned against expecting too much from education alone in the moulding of character.

18

The decision rested, in practice, with Prince Albert, on whom lay the potent influence of Baron Stockmar. The Baron had produced between 1842 and 1848 a series of memoranda on the subject, which stressed the need to give 'a truly moral and a truly English' instruction and to choose good and pure tutors in whom absolute trust could be put to produce a moral, upright monarch. The assumption behind the Stockmar system was that it would be possible to 'engraft' on to the mind of the Prince 'the principles of truth and morality'. Victoria, who had suffered perhaps from the early death of her father and from the hostility shown towards her mother by William IV, was ready to assent to these principles of education, more especially since they were laid down by her darling Albert; and she would have agreed with him that 'the English machine works smoothly ... only when the sovereign is upright and truthful'. Albert himself had been a naturally studious prince and was fully conscious that 'the welfare of the world in these days depended on the good education of princes'; the more so since his son was one day to be the head of state of an empire far greater than any German prince's domain.

'The welfare of the world in these days depended on the good education of princes'

Edward's first tutor was Henry Birch, an assistant master at Eton, who had had a fine academic record at Cambridge. Birch was engaged to head the staff of tutors, while he himself taught the Prince calculating, geography and English. He was instructed to send regular reports on his pupil's progress to Albert and Stockmar and to adhere to the programme of education set down by the royal family. Clearly Edward resented the regime of constant study, involving lesson periods of five hours a day, five days a week, and his resentment was shown in displays of temper and periods of sullenness. Nonetheless, he grew attached to Birch and was genuinely upset when he was replaced.

The new man was a barrister, Frederick Gibbs, whose views were more in tune with those of Albert and Stockmar. The lessons were extended to six hours a day, six days a week. Light reading, which included the novels of Walter Scott, was now forbidden and the hours not devoted to book-learning were spent in a harsh regime of physical exercise. Gibbs himself seems to have been uncongenial to the young Prince: his inflexible attitude may have stemmed from the fact that his own mother had become insane and his father had failed in business. Altogether he made an odd choice for a boy of ten. Edward began to show signs of nervous exhaustion and some observers noticed an air of melancholy which seemed to have become part of his nature. This was at first mistaken by his parents for sobriety, and the system was applauded. In fact, he was temperamentally unsuited to the rigid discipline imposed on him, and both Albert and Stockmar should be blamed for much of his unhappiness. There were criticisms: Dr Becker, one of the assistant tutors, prepared a report condemning the effects of Gibbs's work, but he failed to shake the unyielding attitude of Edward's father and of Stockmar.

*'Such a father …
so great, so good,
so marvellous'*

Among the Hanoverians it was almost traditional that father and son should dislike, or even loathe, each other. The mutual antipathy of George III and his son was well within living memory. But if Edward felt this for Albert, he disguised it skilfully. On the other hand, he certainly suffered as a result of his mother's obvious preference for her more intelligent elder daughter, Vicky. Moreover, none of the children could hope to rouse her affection as much as Albert. 'None of you', she wrote, 'can ever be proud enough of being the child of such a father who has not his equal in this world – so great, so good, so marvellous.' At times Victoria's feelings were almost excessively frank; writing to the Queen of Prussia in 1856, she declared that she found 'no especial pleasure or compensation in the company of the older children'. The Queen was prone to see the evidence of her son's stupidity a little too readily, perhaps because Albert bemoaned the low standard of the entries in the diary that he insisted the Prince kept and showed to him. Edward lacked intellectual leanings and thus he found himself in a vicious circle – the more he failed to satisfy his parents' expectations, the more they felt him as wilful and lacking in intelligence, and the more they felt he was in need of a strong, guiding hand to mould his character.

Isolated as they were within the bounds of court society and brought up as they had been themselves in the company of adults, Victoria and Albert imposed an even more isolated regime on their son. The royal nurseries might be crowded (Victoria had eight children between 1840 and 1857), but the atmosphere was unpolluted by any element from the raucous

RIGHT Osborne House – the home built by Victoria on the Isle of Wight, where Edward spent much of his childhood. When Edward finally became King, he adapted the house into a naval cadet centre.
BELOW Winterhalter's formal portrait, painted in 1846, of Victoria and her family. Edward stands by his mother's knee, Alfred, her second son, stands to the left, while Alice and Vicky, her eldest daughters, rock Helena.

Victoria collected many informal photographs of her children for her personal album. Here, the royal children are seen taking part in a tableau of the seasons in February 1854. Left to right: Alice, Arthur, Vicky, Helena, Alfred, Louise and Edward.

and morally suspect outside world. Edward lived in the company of his father and his family, not of other children. When he was taken around the royal residences, or shown the wonders of the Great Exhibition, he was under constant survey – Albert commented mournfully on the unhealthy interest shown at the Exhibition by a Christian prince in the stand dealing with the activities of the Indian Thugee sect. The pageantry of the opening of Parliament and the pleasures (in moderation) of shooting and hunting were no remedy for the isolation from young people of his own age. Such contact as there was came through the Prince's visits to Eton on prize days and the admission after 1852 of a few hand-picked companions from the schools, who were allowed to take tea with him at Windsor. Even then his father was continually present to see that Edward's behaviour did not grow too 'loose'. It was pressure from Lord Granville which persuaded Albert to make a great concession. In 1856 the Prince was allowed to undertake a walking tour, and the following year he was accompanied by four other boys from

Queen Victoria opening the Great Exhibition at the Crystal Palace in 1851. Edward thoroughly enjoyed this exhibition, and was noted, by his father, to be taking too much interest in the stand dealing with the Thugee sect of India.

OPPOSITE Portrait of Edward in 1858 by R.J. Lane. Edward had visited Paris two years earlier and cut a charming figure in his kilt.

Eton. However, by the mid-50s even Gibbs was mellowing in his view of the effects of the educational system that he had faithfully carried through. In 1854 he pointed out that 'the Prince is a boy, and it is very difficult for older people to say what he should observe and admire'. Gibbs supported the idea of letting the Prince gain some experience of foreign travel, and when the Crimean Alliance was cemented by a visit of the royal family to Paris in August 1856, Edward was allowed to accompany his parents. On the vivid court of the Second Empire, the charming figure of the Prince of Wales in a kilt made a favourable impression, which was reduced to pathos by his request (coming as it did from a boy nearly fifteen years old) to the Empress to allow him to stay in Paris – 'They [his parents] don't want us, and there are six more of us at home.'

Edward's life-long love of travelling grew out of this early experience of the European courts. Tours of Italy in 1859 and of Canada and the United States in 1860 gave him welcome relief from the arid formalities of his life at home, and the relative freedom he enjoyed stimulated a growing sense of independence and maturity. Abroad he found himself, in Louis Blanc's phrase, 'a fairy personage'. Dancing the cotillion in Berlin in 1858 he had his first real experience of gay social life, and he noted in his diary that there was 'plenty of larking' at Gibraltar on his way back from the Italian tour. In New York he became automatically the centre of society revelry and danced until

24

dawn at a magnificent ball given in his honour in October 1860.

Edward not only enjoyed the lighter side of these visits; he began to show a sensitivity to political situations. In America he had to cope tactfully with the tensions between Orange and Catholic Irish factions, and in New York he soon realised that an easing of the stiffness of royal protocol could increase the popularity of monarchy without invoking the dire consequences predicted by his father. In Italy he had spoken with the Pope and met Robert Browning and Lord Leighton, while in America he showed equal facility of conversation with Oliver Wendell Holmes, Emerson and Longfellow. His later charm and diplomacy were already evident.

On his coming of age, at seventeen, in November 1858, Edward was allowed his first taste of independence at home. The White Lodge in Richmond Park was given him for use, but strict supervision was still kept up. Albert laid down rules for the Prince's dress: 'He will ... avoid the frivolity and foolish vanity of dandyism'. His conduct must never include 'anything approaching to a practical joke'. Instead he would permit 'anything that, whilst it amused, may gently exercise the mind'. These instructions were to be administered by a staff of equerries under a 'governor', Colonel Robert Bruce.

While Edward was given an allowance of £500 a year, mainly to buy his own clothes, Victoria cautioned him that 'although we do not wish to control your own tastes ... we do expect that you will never wear anything extravagant. It would ... lead to an indifference to what is morally wrong'. Albert had urged his son to 'try to emancipate yourself as much as possible from the thraldom of abject dependence ... on your servants'; but he also told Bruce to regard himself *in loco parentis* and to restrict the Prince's social activity to the company of sober and responsible adults. Albert also made the decision that the Prince should attend Oxford University, resisting the boy's desire to undergo military training. While at the University, which Albert regarded as 'a place for study, a refuge from the world', Edward should live outside the town, in Frewin Hall, where his contact with other undergraduates would be limited.

But all Albert's efforts could not prevent Edward from developing a taste for social activity, which his foreign travels had already given him, and if Edward was the first sovereign to

matriculate from Oxford since Prince Hal, academic activity had as little inherent attraction to him as it had for his predecessor. Altogether Edward attended three universities, Edinburgh, Oxford and Cambridge, but his contact with scholars such as Lyon Playfair, Dr Henry Liddell, Dr Whewell, Goldwin Smith, or Charles Kingsley, was rather less significant than the friendships he made at Oxford with Henry Chaplin and Frederick Johnstone, and at Cambridge with Nathaniel Rothschild and Charles Beresford.

During these years Edward was developing the tastes for cigars, hunting and the company of 'bloods' that were to provide him with his later public reputation for fast living. It is a tribute to his strength of character, or perhaps to his vestigial respect for the Stockmar system, that he did not become, in reaction to childhood pressures, an out-and-out rake. If he rejected the austerity of his parents, he did not revolt against it in any conscious way. Nevertheless his path was diverging fast from that envisaged by his parents and the explosion was not likely to be delayed. In the summer of 1861 Edward was sent to the Curragh for military education. Albert had refused to consider Aldershot, thinking the moral risks of such a place to be too great; but army customs flourished universally among the

In 1860, Edward made his highly successful tour of the United States and Canada, demonstrating already his charm and diplomacy.
LEFT Engraving, made from a painting by Winterhalter of the eighteen-year-old Prince, which was exclusively distributed in Canada to commemorate his visit.
RIGHT Presentations made to Edward at Government House, Halifax.

The education of the Prince

In 1858, Edward was sent to Oxford University as part of his studies. This was an unprecedented step, as the only previous Prince of Wales said to have attended university was Henry v. It was at Oxford – and later at Cambridge and Edinburgh – that Edward met many of his life-long friends.

BELOW Edward and his tutors at Oxford. From left to right: Colonel Bruce, his 'governor', F.W. Gibbs, his tutor, Prince Edward, and the Reverend Turner, his chaplain.

PUNCH, OR THE LONDON CHARIVARI.—October 29, 1859.

THE ROYAL ROAD TO LEARNING.

ABOVE Frewin Hall, the residence of Edward while at Oxford.

LEFT *Punch*'s comment upon Edward's scholastic career.

29

officer class, and the traditions of the élite owed nothing to more conventional middle-class morality. Edward's desire for army life did not simply imply an eagerness to learn the routines of drill, and, despite the shortness of his stay at the Curragh and the instructions which his father gave to the camp commandant, it was here that an incident occurred that was to throw a pall over the last months of Albert's life – in his own words 'to cause the greatest pain I have yet felt in this life'.

In November 1861, when Edward had returned from Ireland as an ensign and was living at Madingley Hall, Cambridge, Albert heard the rumour that a liaison had been carried on at the Curragh between his son and an actress, one Nellie Clifden. Confronted with the story, Edward was tactful enough to admit that he had 'yielded to temptation' and to assure his father that the affair was over. (This was not strictly true. In 1862 Edward was apparently still infatuated with Nellie.) Albert's warning to his son reflected his belief that such behaviour could only bring the position of the monarchy into danger. 'You must not, you dare not be lost. The consequences for the country, for the world, would be too dreadful!' The Prince Consort hastened his plans to send the Prince of Wales on a tour of the Near East and on 25 November came down to Madingley Hall for a talk with his son. All seemed forgiven (not for nothing did Poincaré once attribute Edward's diplomatic skill to his early experience in handling his parents), but during his stay at Cambridge Albert contracted a chill. In two weeks he was dying of typhoid fever. A year of personal sorrow for Victoria's family was crowned by the death of Albert on 14 December 1861 at Windsor. In the first agony of grief, despite the sorrow and devotion displayed by Edward at the death-bed of his father, Victoria remembered only too clearly the role which her son's conduct had played. 'Oh, that boy,' she wrote. 'Much as I pity, I never can, or shall, look at him without a shudder.'

OPPOSITE 'Day turned into night': the mourning of the Queen and her children at the sudden death of Albert in December 1861.

2
The
Public
Path
of
the

Prince of
Wales
1861-1901

ICH DIEN

So SINCERE WAS Edward's unhappiness at his father's death and so tactful his response to his mother's grief, that her initial repulsion was dispelled. Nevertheless, Victoria's reaction to the loss of Albert was to dominate her remaining years. She interpreted her future duty as service to Albert's memory. What he had advised or striven for was to be her own desire; his labours should fall upon her shoulders. Assistance from anyone alive 'be he ever so good, ever so devoted' was seen as unimportant. The Prince Consort's wishes, as construed by his widow, were instead given the authority of holy writ.

As far as her eldest son was concerned, this attitude meant that the plans already made for him should be carried out as soon as possible. The Near East tour, intended to distract him from the memory of Nellie Clifden, should take place; and the projected plans for his marriage should be brought to a successful conclusion.

The Near East tour provided evidence of his growing ability to conduct himself abroad with independence and diplomatic success. He impressed the members of his entourage and the British ambassador in Constantinople, Sir Henry Bulwer, who noted his tactful handling of the Sultan. Laurence Oliphant, whom he met in Austria, declared that 'his development will be higher than people anticipate'. One sadness occurred, cutting a link with the past – General Bruce fell ill and died. Soon, with the complicated overtures preceding a royal marriage, the remaining ties with his restricted youth were threatened.

Prince Albert had decided that Edward should marry young and there was no doubt that he would marry into the royal caste. Even in July 1858, at the time of his coming of age, as many as seven young princesses were, according to *The Times*, under consideration. Alexandra of Schleswig-Holstein-Sonderburg-Glucksburg, a daughter of the relatively poor Danish royal family, came fifth on the list. Her candidature, however, was backed by Princess Victoria of Prussia (Edward's eldest sister, Vicky), who had married the future German Emperor, Frederick III, in 1858.

Edward was determined that he should have some say in the matter of his future partner and soon rejected the idea of Elizabeth of Wied, whose photographs did not meet with his approval. In September 1861 a meeting with Alexandra in the

PREVIOUS PAGE Portrait of Edward and Sandringham House, his favourite home, in the 1860s.

34

A family gathering at Windsor on the eve of Edward's marriage to Alexandra. From left to right: Prince Christian of Denmark, Princess Christian, their son Prince Frederick, Princess Alice, Crown Prince of Prussia, Prince Louis of Hesse, Princess Helena, Princess Alexandra, Prince of Wales, Crown Princess of Prussia, Prince William of Denmark, Princess Dagmar, Princess Louise.

cathedral of Speyer produced a favourable impression, to the delight of Princess Victoria, who had arranged it. After the death of Albert, Queen Victoria, who had gone to Coburg to visit the childhood home of her husband, saw the Danish Princess for herself and on this occasion Edward, who had accompanied his mother, proposed 'after a few commonplace remarks'. 'I only feared', he wrote, afterwards, 'that I was not worthy of her.' He was immediately accepted. Victoria, however, still had some reservations. While she was happy that the marriage was said to be a love match, she wanted to make it quite clear that the union was 'in no way connected with political considerations'.

Such tact was needed because of the growing dispute over the inheritance of the duchies of Schleswig-Holstein, claimed on one side by the Danish Crown, under the terms of the 1842 Convention of London, and on the other by the young Duke of Augustenburg, whose case was backed by the power of Prussia, Austria and the German Confederation. The last thing Queen Victoria desired was that her son should be drawn into what ultimately became a *casus belli* between the two sides. Already the Duke of Saxe-Coburg opposed the match, and the Queen insisted on having Alexandra over to Windsor on a private visit, during which she could warn the Princess 'of the danger of using her influence to make the Prince a partisan'. The Princess's father had to stay in a London hotel during the period of this vital interview, and Edward was despatched on a tour of the Mediterranean. Despite the overawing circumstances, Alexandra handled the Queen with superb skill and in the end

LEFT Edward and Alexandra with Victoria – and the spirit of Albert – an hour after their marriage.
BELOW Marlborough House, the London home of the Prince and Princess of Wales, in about 1860.

Victoria hailed her future daughter-in-law as 'one of those sweet creatures who seem to come from the skies to help and bless poor mortals'. 'How beloved Albert would have loved her', she recorded in her diary, and in April 1863 she visited the Frogmore mausoleum, where he was buried, with the couple; and she declared, 'He gives you his blessing'. The accolade indeed!

The marriage was a popular one. Tennyson wrote of the bride, with more sensibility than style:

> Sea King's daughter as happy as fair
> Blissful bride of a blissful heir

OPPOSITE The wedding of Edward and Alexandra, 10 March 1863, at St George's Chapel, Windsor. The Queen, still in complete mourning for Albert, insisted on watching the service from a special box, on the right of the picture. Detail from a painting by Frith.

Those who were not touched by Alexandra's beauty and the obvious affection between the handsome young couple, could welcome, as did Lady Palmerston, the leavening of the Germanic element in the royal family. The wedding took place on 10 March 1863, in St George's Chapel, Windsor, somewhat out of the public gaze, but bonfires were lit throughout Britain in celebration of the event. After a short honeymoon at Osborne, the Prince and Princess moved into Marlborough House,

*'He should be early
initiated ... the
more confidence we
show in him, the
better it will be'*

which had been prepared since 1850 at great expense as a residence for the Prince's maturity.

Parliament had now to consider the question of Edward's income, and Lord Palmerston, the Prime Minister, was able to offer the sum of £40,000 a year, with an additional £10,000 a year for Alexandra. This vote was passed through the House of Commons without a division. To it was added the income from the duchy of Cornwall estates, whose revenues, under the governing hand of Albert, had produced some £50,000 a year, and the receipt of £7,000 a year from the rent roll of the Sandringham property. It is, however, worth noting that this sum represented a decrease of about £15,000 a year on the income of George III's successor, and that no further increases were voted by Parliament until his succession in 1901 (with the exception of the marriage allowances granted to his sons in 1889). Consequently, Edward's expenditure sometimes fell short of the Micawberish ideal and, even if the deficit seldom exceeded £20,000 in any one year, it was only through the advice of financier friends, like the Rothschilds, Maurice Hirsch and Ernest Cassel, that he was able to live the life of a nineteenth-century aristocrat to the full. It was fortunate that many of his travels (notably those to Ireland, Russia and India) were to some extent subsidised by the government.

Now that he was practically, as well as formally, independent, what kind of life was the Prince of Wales expected to lead? Clearly, marriage and financial security had put him beyond the immediate supervision of his mother, but it was not immediately obvious whether he was destined to lead a career similar to that of earlier Hanoverian princes or to follow the example of the Prince Consort and play an important and responsible role in the councils of the State. After Albert's death, many people expected that all the functions of Victoria's partner would devolve on his son. There were even rumours that the Queen would abdicate in Edward's favour. But these were far from the mark and the Prince of Wales entered into the long period, spanning nearly forty years, during which, although heir apparent to the throne, he was denied all real power and influence in political life. The decision that this should be so was very largely a conscious one taken by Queen Victoria. She remembered too clearly the opinion of Albert as to the capabilities of their eldest son and allowed this to override her own awareness that, since Edward would one day succeed her, he ought therefore to be given some experience of affairs of state. When Edward was only nine, she had written: 'He should be early initiated ... the more confidence we show in him, the better it will be'; yet this judgement was evidently vitiated by later circumstances. As a result, by her refusal to consider Edward fitted to carry out any of the functions of the late Prince Consort, and by her own withdrawal from London and the public gaze, the Queen made it impossible for Edward to develop his character in the sobering business of following the strands of government.

As early as 1862 Laurence Oliphant had stated that the Prince's defects of character were due to 'a position which never allowed him responsibility, or forces him into action'. The authority of the sovereign remained vested solely in Victoria and the vagueness of Edward's position in the constitutional structure was to obstruct him whenever he tackled a question of political importance. His frustration was partially due to Victoria's own egoism; but there was also some justification for the Queen's disquiet about his conduct in society and for her complaints about the choice of his companions, his lack of discretion and his predilection for the advice of certain unwelcome individuals. Everyone who has written of the Prince of Wales's career is unanimous about the effects of the lack of organised work, but it is noticeable that Edward himself did not seek out the more arduous responsibilities which his father had been only too willing to undertake. True, Edward wished to be informed on certain issues in which he was interested and was resentful when access to this information was denied, but nothing in his behaviour during his youth indicated his father's appetite for serious application to the problems of State.

'The Prince has been more than usually unwise in his talk'

Moreover, quite clear differences over foreign policy emerged between Victoria and her son. In spite of the attempts to put the marriage beyond politics, during the Danish-Prussian War over Schleswig-Holstein, Edward took the side of his wife and sympathised with the Danish cause. Honestly but unwisely, he made no secret of his position, even when talking to the French ambassador. All Victoria's instincts were with the other side and she informed Lord John Russell, the Foreign Secretary, that the Prince was not to enter into any independent contact with the Cabinet. She sympathised with the Prince's wish to do so, but could not 'help objecting to the principle' of separate and independent communication with her ministers, fearing that 'great inconvenience, not to say injury, might be occasioned'. Edward, who felt that 'a great outcry will occur if we don't do something or other', was probably closer to the feeling of the country on this issue than Victoria, but his offer to act as an intermediary between the British Government and the Danish royal family was refused.

Afterwards the only information on foreign affairs available to him was such as he could garner from the press and private contacts. Despite the willingness to discuss problems with him of such statesmen as Gladstone, who gave him in 1870 the doubtful privilege of a two-hour conversation on the subject of his Irish policy, and despite Disraeli's grant of a key to the box containing Cabinet papers, it was not until 1892 that Edward was in full possession of all relevant Government information. As late as 1885, during the Afghanistan crisis, he was complaining to Victoria that 'needless to say … I am kept in perfect ignorance as to what is going on'. He came to look with some envy on the position of Prince Leopold, who served the Queen as a private secretary, and in consequence was forced to lean heavily on the reports of his friends who held posts in the Government, notably Lord Hartington, Sir Henry James, Lord Rosebery and Sir Charles Dilke. Victoria's distrust of her son continued. During the Franco-Prussian War she refused his offer to visit the King of Prussia with a view to ending the conflict; his desire might be 'highly creditable' but he was not 'personally fitted for such a very difficult task'. The reason was not hard to find: at the beginning of the war Edward had declared his hope that France would win, and even Granville noted 'the Prince has been more than usually unwise in his talk'.

Division between Edward and Victoria was heightened by the fact that his activities revolved round the public aspects of the monarchy, from which Victoria had withdrawn on the death of her husband. Against her charges that his mode of life brought him into disrepute, Edward retorted: 'We have certain duties to fulfil here [in London] and your absence … makes it more necessary that we should do all we can for

'I have now been of age for some time and am alone *responsible'*

40

society, trade and public matters.' Court levées and late night parties at Marlborough House were among Victoria's complaints. Yet Edward filled many of the posts graced by his father. He became President of the Society of Arts, Chairman of the Governors of Wellington College, and in 1870 the Chairman of the Commission dealing with Albert's own South Kensington project. The round of public functions which the Prince undertook was no mean task; the opening of buildings, including the London Hospital and Glasgow University, and the giving of banquet speeches, increased in number until in about the 1880s he was undertaking some forty-two functions a year. These activities may have been relatively trivial (although the Prince did some valuable work as one of the Trustees of the British Museum, in the course of which he became a firm convert to the idea of Sunday opening of museums) but they filled the void of inactivity which otherwise might have been unbearable. Edward became a firm believer in the value of exhibitions and participated in a number of such characteristically nineteenth-century displays as the International Fisheries Exhibition and the Colonies and Indian Exhibition. He was also a prime mover in the setting up of the Imperial Institute during the Jubilee celebrations of 1887 and a lifelong supporter of various medical charities.

But his more overtly political activities frequently incurred his mother's wrath. When Edward visited Garibaldi privately during the Italian patriot's visit to London in 1864, Victoria scolded General Knollys (Comptroller-General of the Prince's household), instructing him that 'no step of the slightest political importance shall be taken without due consultation with the Queen'. But Edward was able to show an independent streak and disclaimed any direct responsibility. He wrote to Knollys: 'I have now been of age for some time and am *alone* responsible.' Similarly, when Victoria wrote to Edward expressing her concern that her son was so heavily involved in pursuits of dubious moral value – racing, shooting and so on – he replied, caustically, that he disliked her continual 'jobiation'. 'I am past twenty-eight ... allow me to use my own discretion.'

Victoria worried not only about these social activities, but because she thought her son was prone to involvement in party politics. True, Edward had flirted with the Conservative

The public path of the
Prince and Princess of
Wales.
RIGHT Edward unveiling
a marble statue of his
mother at Aberdeen in
1866.
BELOW The opening
ceremony of Tower
Bridge in 1894.

opposition during the Schleswig-Holstein War, partly out of disgust at the inactivity of the Government, and partly because the Cabinet denied him information, in compliance with Victoria's wishes. On the other hand, he really had little interest in either political party, or in coherent political philosophies. While his friends and staff tended towards a Liberal outlook, Edward was basically Conservative in his attitude to domestic affairs. He urged Charles Carrington, unsuccessfully, to vote against the Reform Bill of 1866, and considered that Gladstone's prolonged concessions to the Irish were useless. He seems actually to have believed that 'the safety of the crown itself' was endangered by the attack on the Anglican Establishment in Ireland and he lamented the lack of firm Government action against the demonstrations that were becoming increasingly popular. 'The more the Government allows the lower classes to get the upper hand, the more the democratic feeling will increase.'

But social activity was usually more important to Edward than the procedure of political debate, and he tended to consider a case less on its merits than on the personalities of those who advocated it. The 'jingoistic sentiments' which were noted by Dilke, owed more to his contacts with Disraeli or Bartle Frere and to personal admiration of men like General Gordon, Cecil Rhodes and Dr Jameson than to any profound belief in imperialism. He crossed party lines without being conscious of distinctions. Influenced by Liberal friends like Lord Rosebery, he gave his support to the proposals of the Third Reform Bill, and during the crisis following the Bill's rejection by the Lords, he received the plaudits of the crowds demonstrating in London. Thus, no party leader went out of his way to antagonise the Prince. Edward remained on excellent terms with the Prime Ministers Gladstone, Disraeli and Salisbury successively, and there was never anything to compare with the Prince of Wales's Party of the previous century – further evidence, perhaps, of the decreasing importance of the Crown in politics. On the two notable occasions when Gladstone did use the Prince's influence – when Edward urged on his mother the need to summon Gladstone to form a government in 1880, and again in 1882 when he persuaded the reluctant Lord Rosebery to join Gladstone's fourth administration – he was merely hastening

43

what was almost inevitable. The best and only real effect of Edward's political independence was that he prevented the Crown from assuming too rigid a party attitude, as Victoria threatened to do during the years when she was obsessed with her fear of the 'dreadful old man' – Gladstone. As Granville noted, the result of the Prince's visit to Garibaldi was not to compromise the monarchy, but to 'take the democratic sting out of the affair'.

Edward took his seat in the House of Lords on 4 February 1863 and attended its sittings quite frequently. None of his speeches betrayed any party bias and his early activities were limited to work on innocuous House of Lords Committees into the Cattle Plague and the Supply of Horses – subjects hardly calculated to arouse either much interest or much political argument. He was involved in the passage of the two bills which aimed at legalising the marriage of a widower to his deceased wife's sister; defeated in the 1870s, the bill finally reached the Statute Book in 1896 and the Archbishop of Canterbury, who had opposed it, together with nearly all the bishops, attributed its success to the Prince's influence in persuading so many sporting 'backwoodsmen' to come and vote it through.

More important questions came within the scope of the Royal Commission into the Housing of the Working Classes, which the Prince joined as a member in 1884, at Gladstone's invitation. The subject was one of vital concern to the social conscience of late Victorian England and, under the aegis of the Commission, Edward met such figures as Cardinal Manning, Lord Salisbury, George Goschen, Sir Richard Cross, Jesse Collings and the Chairman, Sir Charles Dilke. He visited the slums of St Pancras and Clerkenwell and was genuinely horrified by the conditions found there. But family distractions, notably the death of Prince Leopold, prevented him from attending more than nineteen of the fifty-one meetings held in 1884. He signed part of the Report and was clearly sympathetic to its tenor. In his speech in the Lords he mentioned his own work in the creation of a model estate at Sandringham. Yet he must have been conscious that much of the slum property in South London was owned by the duchy of Cornwall, a fact that he admitted at the opening of Bethnal Green Museum in 1900, when he pointed out that he was powerless to affect the

OPPOSITE The Prince of Wales delivering his first speech in the House of Lords in February 1884, from a water-colour by F. Walter Wilson

condition of property which was mostly leased by the duchy rather than directly managed by it.

Edward wished also to serve on the Royal Commission on Labour in 1891, but his request was refused by Lord Salisbury on the grounds that the nature of its work would necessarily make it divide on party lines. Later he was offered a place on the Royal Commission on the Aged Poor. The Commission sat for two years and the record of the Prince's attendance was more regular. The Commission divided and Edward felt unable to put his name to the Report, but his presence gave weight to the proceedings, coming as they did at a time when the question of old age pensions was assuming some importance. Among his colleagues on the Commission were Henry Broadhurst, the first working man to become a Cabinet minister, and Joseph Arch, founder of the first stable Trades Union among agricultural workers. With both of these Edward developed friendship, inviting Broadhurst to Sandringham, and giving his support to Arch's attempts to secure election to Parliament as a member for the Norfolk constituency that included Sandringham.

Although such work widened his social horizons and involved him, at more than just a superficial level, in the social concerns of the age, it came at a time when the powers of the monarchy were in decline. Edward's attitudes to burning political questions, such as the Bulgarian agitation of the late 1870s, which he 'deeply deplored', and Home Rule (which he, like his Liberal Unionist friends, dismissed as unwise in theory and impossible in political terms) tended to be expressed in private and carried little weight with those actually involved in the political decisions. The Queen's own power to appoint or dismiss ministers was diminishing despite the prestige of her fifty years of rule, and the Prince of Wales was much less able to impose his views. In 1898, when the lord chamberlainship fell vacant, he proved incapable of securing the appointment for his nominee, Lord Pembroke. The things he did appear to accomplish – the appointment of Campbell-Bannerman as Secretary for War in 1886, the refusal to accept Count Toricelli as Italian ambassador in 1896 – were due more to their appositeness at the time than to his own advocacy. Indeed, some of his proposals during the formation of the Liberal ministry of 1892 –

'This present Prince should never dishonour his country by becoming its king . . .'

46

that Carrington should become Viceroy of India and that Mrs Gladstone should be given a peerage – were rejected out of hand by the Prime Minister. Royal displeasure counted for less than in the past, and during the period of his quarrel with Lord Randolph Churchill, Edward was unable to affect Churchill's political career, whatever the damage he dealt to his social life.

On one major issue, however, the Crown itself became the object of political conflict. By the late 1860s it appeared intensely unpopular. Republicanism, a force lacking in Britain in any appreciable sense since the seventeenth century, was now something to be reckoned with. The Queen's behaviour was partly responsible. She had become, to all intents and purposes, a recluse. Writing to her from Egypt during his long tour of the Mediterranean during 1868–9, Edward added his voice to those who pointed out that 'we live in radical times and the more the *people see the sovereign*, the better it is for the *people* and the *country*'. The absence of pomp and ceremony, and the more ridiculous aspects of the Queen's attachment to her Scots ghillie, John Brown, were criticised by the daily press and by *Punch*, and in scurrilous pamphlets such as *Mrs John Brown*. There was widespread resentment that the Queen was amassing a fortune out of her Civil List, while her expenditure remained minimal. 'What does she do with it?' the pamphlets asked. The attacks widened their target and for quite different reasons lighted on the Prince of Wales. Charles Bradlaugh had attacked his way of living in his *Letter from a free-mason to General H.R.H. Albert Edward, Prince of Wales*, which, it has been suggested, was so near to the mark that it was responsible for Edward's long absence from the country in 1868–9. Objection was taken not to the Prince's piling up of funds, but to his too liberal use of what was allotted to him; combined with this was an attempt to dissect the character of the future King. At the height of the republican campaign, Bradlaugh launched a fierce indictment of Edward's record. 'This present Prince should never dishonour his country by becoming its king … neither his intelligence nor his virtues … can entitle him to occupy the throne of Great Britain.' Pamphlets with titles like *Guelpho the Gay* and *The Coming K* purported to strip the veil from the Prince's private life, and one called *The Infidelities of a Prince* recalled the unfortunate example of George IV.

'Neither his intelligence nor his virtues … can entitle him to occupy the throne'

47

Charles Dilke (top) and Joseph Chamberlain, two leading politicians involved in the attack on the monarchy in the late 1860s and early 1870s. Later they both became close friends of the Prince of Wales.

OPPOSITE Max Beerbohm's cartoon of the relationship between Victoria and Edward.

The climax of the campaign was reached in 1871, the year of the Mordaunt scandal. Republicanism flourished in the aftermath of the French Republic and the *Pall Mall Gazette* hinted that the neutrality of the royal family had been compromised during the Franco-Prussian War by communication with the King and Crown Princess of Prussia. Charles Dilke and Joseph Chamberlain were among those involved in the attack on the institution of monarchy, and there were riotous scenes at a large republican meeting in London on 16 April 1871. Republican clubs sprang up all over the country and Dilke proclaimed: 'I say for my part – and I believe that the middle classes will say: "Let it, [the republic] come"'. Chamberlain concurred, 'The republic must come'. Hostile demonstrations were made against Edward at the Olympia Theatre and at Ascot in June he was booed as he drove to the course. Gladstone himself felt that, although 'for my time as a politician, royalty will do well enough', the fund of credit the monarchy could call on was diminishing. He noted the Prince of Wales's 'negative position as to duty' and feared for the future. 'The Queen is invisible and the Prince of Wales is not respected.'

The royal circle refused to budge. Edward continued to chide his mother for her lack of public appearances and she rebuked him for his fast living and choice of companions – in particular objecting to his choice of Francis Knollys to fill the place of his personal secretary. Faced with the hostile reaction of the Ascot crowd, the Prince retained his good spirits and after his horses had won some of the races he exclaimed on the way home, 'You seem to be in a better temper now ... damn you!' He continued to read *Reynold's News*, the popular newspaper that had once printed the sentence 'The Heir Apparent was staking his gold upon the chances of a card or the roll of a ball – gold that he obtained from the toil and sweat of the British working man'.

In the event the republican agitation was destroyed – partly as a result of the horrors of the Paris Commune and the difficult experiences of the infant Third Republic, but mainly because of the sympathy aroused by Edward's serious illness at the end of the year. Typhoid, contracted from the bad drains at Londesborough Lodge, struck him down at the end of October and by December his doctors believed him to be on his deathbed. As Victoria sat beside him, she no doubt recalled the sad

48

The rare, the rather awful visits of Albert Edward, Prince of Wales, to Windsor Castle.

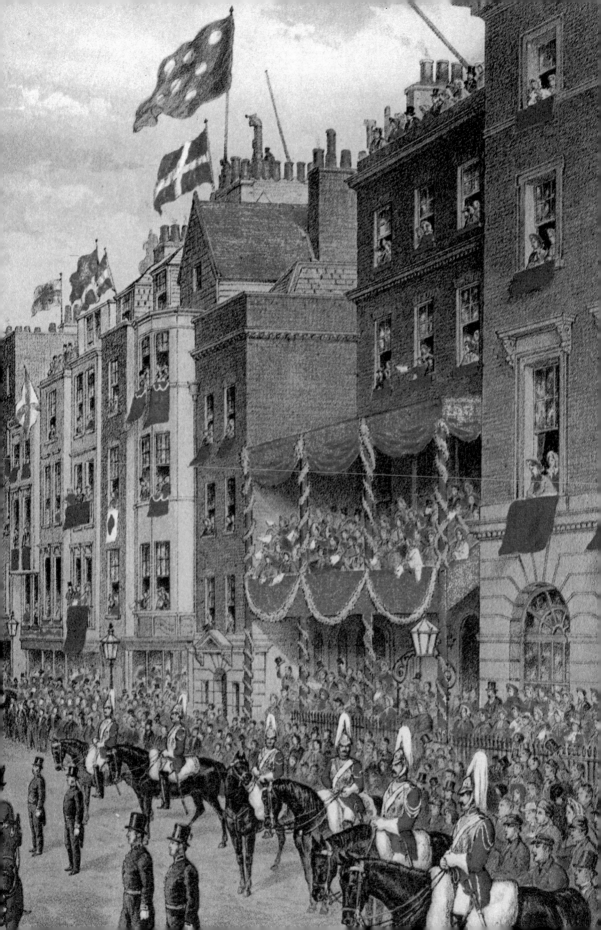

PREVIOUS PAGES
The wedding procession
of Edward and Alexandra,
1863. The procession is
passing through Temple
Bar on its way to
Windsor.

significance of 14 December; but on this day the Prince survived the major crisis and, apart from one relapse, grew steadily better. On 27 February 1872, the Prince and the Queen (who had realised how dear Bertie was to her, despite his many faults) drove together to a thanksgiving service at St Paul's, attended by thirteen thousand people. The applause from the crowd that lined the route suggested that the fund of goodwill was far from exhausted. A month later Dilke failed to obtain an inquiry into the royal finances.

Of course criticism continued. It was impossible to think of asking Parliament to increase Edward's allowance, even though his debts in 1874 were estimated to run to £600,000. Hostile pamphlets appeared with regularity – *The Siliad*, *Jon Duan* (1875), *Phisto* (1874), *Edward* VII (a play of seven acts, published in 1876) – but Gladstone wisely told Granville that proceedings against them would merely give them undue publicity. Edward himself did something to undermine organised republicanism by making friends with some of its leaders. In July 1870 he was welcomed at the opening of the Trades Union-organised Workers' International Exhibition by Auberon Herbert, a declared republican, and it seems that his presence could exert an appeal that was hard to explain in rational terms. In 1874 Edward ventured into the Birmingham citadel of Joseph Chamberlain and was greeted, not with the fire and thunder of yore, but with a declaration by the mayor that 'here in England the throne is recognised and respected as the symbol of all constitutional authority and settled government'. By 1880 both Chamberlain and Dilke had been invited to Marlborough House and Dilke entered into a period of amity with the Prince that lasted even after his disgrace in the divorce suit of 1885. In any case, republicanism had little strength left after its climax. By April 1872, so astute a politician as Benjamin Disraeli was making political capital by proclaiming the wisdom of 'placing the supreme power without the sphere of human passions' and declaring the virtues of a monarchy as 'an intelligence superior to Party'. 'The nation', he continued, 'rallies round the family and the throne and its spirit is animated and sustained by the expression of public affection.' The expressions of enthusiasm during the Jubilee celebrations of 1887 confirmed the validity of Disraeli's hypothesis.

'The nation rallies round the family and the throne'

The crisis of 1870–2, however, was much the strongest attack on the throne since the days of George IV, and it served in the long run to bring the institution into line with the rest of the reformed constitution. The Crown's power was limited: in spite of the long years of Victoria, it was not above the storms of public opinion. More immediately, the crisis led to discussions about the future of the Prince of Wales. Gladstone became convinced that Edward must be found worthwhile work that would 'frame ... a manly mode of life, *quoad* public duties'. His concern was 'to try and frame some plan under which the Prince, before the habits of his mind and life become, so to speak, rigid, shall be provided with some fair share, not of political responsibility, but of public duty'. The plan was that the Prince should take up residence in Ireland and should function there as the Queen's representative, displacing, in effect, the Viceroy. Gladstone's idea had much to recommend it, as it would have provided Edward with valuable administrative experience without involving him in the direct political responsibilities of the Secretary of State for Ireland. The Prince had visited Ireland several times, usually for the Irish racing season at Punchestown, and his receptions had generally been friendly. The Duke of Cambridge was in favour, as were Lord Granville and the Prince's household officers. The Queen was not. She pointed out that Ireland was perhaps the most troubled part of the United Kingdom. Fenianism was rampant and an attempt had been made by Fenians on the life of the Duke of Edinburgh, Edward's brother, whilst on a tour of New South Wales. Given the Prince's natural inclination towards party alignments – in this case the pro-Orange family of the Duke of Abercorn – Victoria thought that the difficulties of the Irish situation would lead him to favour extremes. Her opposition would have been sufficient to blight the chances of the plan in any case, but Edward himself declined. In March 1872, Henry Ponsonby (the Queen's private secretary) informed Gladstone that the Prince 'was even more opposed than the Queen to going in any official capacity to Ireland' and Francis Knollys noted that Edward was not keen on his future being decided without his own consent. Suggestions that a royal residence for him should be provided in Ireland came up again as late as 1885; and even after he came to the throne Edward considered

'The Prince ... shall be provided with some fair share ... of public duty'

Edward in a group at Homburg, one of the spas which the Prince returned to throughout his life. On his right is his cousin, the Duke of Cambridge, the Commander-in-Chief of the British army.

sending his son, George, to that troubled island in some representative capacity – but these plans were also rejected.

His own suggestion that he should be 'successively attached' to each of the Government offices in Whitehall met with little favour. A similar scheme for him to be shown selected Foreign Office documents for comment was rejected because of the administrative delays it would cause, the possibility of his growing resentful when his ideas were not implemented, and the continuing doubts as to his discretion. Ponsonby recalled his experience during the Franco-Prussian War when he had acceded to Edward's demands for information: 'One evening I got four messages from different friends ... one of my first notes to him had been handed round a dinner party!' Since the Prince was apparently uninterested in what documents were sent to him, Disraeli cut off the supply in October 1876 and it is perhaps significant that the person most disappointed when Gladstone gave up his efforts to find employment for Edward was the Prince's secretary, rather than the Prince himself.

Another possibility might have been to involve Edward in military affairs, in which he always showed a lively interest. Having been created an unattached Colonel in 1858 and a General in 1862, he had been genuinely delighted to become Regimental Colonel of the 10th Hussars and Captain-General

54

and Colonel of the Honorable Artillery Company, in succession to his father, in 1863. He developed excellent relations with the Commander-in-Chief, the Duke of Cambridge, who had noted the pleasure he derived from taking part in the military manoeuvres of 1870 – despite his misfortune in being captured with his regiment on the last day. However, the Prince's brothers, the Dukes of Connaught and Edinburgh, were already involved in military careers, and it was commonly thought that the Prince's training had been too hasty to endow him with any real military ability. The sceptics suggested that his interest was centred on questions of army uniform rather than combat, strategy and training. Despite his promotion to Field Marshal in 1875 and to the position of Colonel-in-Chief of the Household Cavalry in 1880, Edward was refused permission to accompany his regiment during the Egyptian campaign of 1882. Granville concurred in the Queen's veto. The Prince could not expect to take part in actual fighting and would lose dignity if he was present as a mere spectator.

In later years, Edward was very sensitive to the comments of his nephew, the Kaiser, that his military activities were confined

Punch's comment upon Edward's position of Captain-General and Colonel of the Honourable Artillery Company. Edward's frustrated military activities were laughed at by many, including the Kaiser.

to the Battle of Flowers in Cannes. The sceptics of his abilities were probably right – Edward tended to see military affairs in a highly personal light. He opposed the reforming plans of General Wolseley when they clashed with the diehard opinions of the Duke of Cambridge, and in 1895 he did his utmost to see that the Duke of Connaught, and not Wolseley, succeeded the ancient Duke as Commander-in-Chief. This effort was fruitless, fortunately for the future of the army, and the Prince found himself in military as in domestic political questions an involved but impotent spectator.

The only other area of government open to him, in which he showed a continued interest when Prince of Wales, was the conduct of foreign affairs. Although he lacked a formal position and although the power of the Crown to direct foreign policy was declining in this field as much as in domestic affairs, Edward formed an opinion on every European crisis and sought to bring it to the attention of the government of the day. His love of travelling gave him some experience of foreign countries, chiefly of France, but also of Germany and Austria during his visits to the spas of Homburg and Marienbad. Moreover, since the European monarchies still maintained a close control over their respective foreign policies, contact between Edward and other sovereigns, most of whom were his relations, could be used as an alternative and sometimes useful channel of communication by the British Government. There were things that could be said more easily by one cousin to another, than at diplomatic level.

Queen Victoria's unwillingness to travel meant that Edward might either entertain visiting heads of State, like Sultan Abdul Aziz in 1867 or the Czar of Russia in 1895, or be sent abroad as the family representative at various court functions. He made three trips to Russia alone in 1866, 1874 and 1894. Travelling might also take him to the colonies, and Sir Charles Phipps paid tribute to his early tour of Canada and the United States as 'one of the most important and valuable State measures of the present age ... impossible to overrate the importance of the good results'. Bartle Frere believed that the Indian tour of 1875–6 had done much to increase the loyalties of both Indian princes and the common people to the British Crown. But if it was one thing to appear before British subjects as the embodiment of the prestige of the royal family, it was quite another to be in a situation where personal action could influence diplomatic events involving the fate of nations.

Undoubtedly foreign observers imagined that the Prince of Wales held more power than was really the case. During the 1860s, when Edward's anti-Prussianism was strongly influenced by the feelings of his wife, the French ambassador, Prince de la Tour d'Auvergne, had given him a good deal of high-level information on the course of events, from French sources. Edward's behaviour was inevitably taken as an indication of British policy and the Queen was therefore anxious that his visits to Denmark and Russia should be balanced by contact with Prussian royalty. Similarly, the Government felt itself involved when in 1870 the Prince made statements of his hopes that the French would smash the Prussians, and instructed him to mollify Prussian sensibilities in private conversation by proclaiming his neutrality. In 1871, he duly went out of his way (and no doubt against his inclination) to be genial to the visiting Crown Prince of Prussia.

Edward's freedom of action in dealing with foreign heads of State was strictly limited by his acceptance of the need to conform to the interests of British diplomacy as conceived by the Foreign Office, and by his regard for Victoria's own opinions as British head of State. When the views of the Prince coincided with those of the Foreign Secretary, his contacts could be useful. Thus, in 1878, Edward made personal contact with the French radical Léon Gambetta, in order to try to mollify his irritation at Britain's acquisition of Cyprus during the Congress of Berlin. In this instance, Lord Salisbury paid tribute to what he had done. In 1881, Charles Dilke had allowed him to meet Jules Ferry, French Finance Minister, and briefed him with the details of the current negotiations for an Anglo-French commercial treaty. On at least one occasion Lord Beaconsfield used royal hostility as an excuse to avoid entering into an unwelcome situation: in 1879 Count Munster, bearing tentative offers of an Anglo-German alliance, had to report to Bismarck that the reasons for rejection included the pro-French sympathies of the heir apparent.

In reality, of course, such considerations were unimportant. Edward stood a few steps removed from the decision-making

'There were things that could be said more easily by one cousin to another'

process, and although he could glean much information from his contacts with French politicians, and although British ministers often talked to him privately about particular issues, there was no formal link with the Foreign Office until the late 1890s. When Rosebery was Foreign Secretary the Prince was sent a selection of Foreign Office despatches, and in 1887 the Under-Secretary, Sir Julian Pauncefote, was still sending him 'all the despatches of real interest ... he should see what cards are in the hands of the players in the great European game'. But Henry Ponsonby, at the Queen's request, put a stop to this. Even in the 1890s, the Prince was complaining to Lord Salisbury that he was not being provided with information on the Greek-Turkish War.

Open rifts of policy with Victoria in the early days resolved themselves later into differences of approach. The more outrageous actions of Kaiser William II were condemned by Victoria as well as her son – especially when the German Emperor refused to allow Edward to attend the Austrian army manoeuvres with him in 1889. Yet she wrote shrewdly enough to Salisbury: 'As regards the political relations of the two Governments, the Queen quite agrees that they should not be affected (if possible) by these miserable personal quarrels.' After the Kaiser had sent his telegram congratulating President Kruger on the failure of the Jameson Raid in 1896, the Prince wrote to his mother that only a 'good snubbing' would be sufficient to deal with such a case. Victoria, who perhaps came into contact with the All-Highest less frequently than did her son, was prepared to be more tolerant, but the ill treatment of the Dowager Empress Victoria after the death of Frederick III made her very angry. However, the bad relations between the Queen and the Kaiser were not allowed to interfere with the negotiations which culminated in the Anglo-German colonial agreement of 1890.

Direct rebuke was limited now to 'snubbing' and this treaty, which ceded Heligoland in return for concessions in Africa and Asia, was ratified by a note in Parliament instead of by the royal signature alone – a precedent which royalty found distasteful. Only on one occasion did Edward go directly against Salisbury's advice – and in that his efforts were quite productive. During the Anglo-American crisis over Venezuela in 1895, Joseph

'These miserable personal quarrels'

58

Pulitzer wrote to Edward asking him to make a statement that would calm an inflamed public opinion. The Prince showed his draft reply to Salisbury, who advised him not to send it; nevertheless Edward went ahead and his message was published in the *New York Times* on Christmas Eve. It played a notable part in taking the tension out of the situation.

Edward's views on foreign policy were never consistent enough to have allowed him to have any deep influence on policy-making. His reactions were often influenced by close associations and personal feelings. His views of Anglo-Russian relations, for example, veered between attempts to encourage friendship in the 1860s to a belief that war was inevitable in the 1870s and back again to the policy of cordiality during the last decade of the nineteenth century. In this it is not hard to trace first the influence of his wife and her private secretary, Sir Maurice Holzmann, succeeded by friendship with Disraeli, and then by his contact with Lord Randolph Churchill and his dislike of the Kaiser. Sometimes his diplomatic efforts were a product of purely family considerations – he constantly supported his brother-in-law, King George of Greece, both at the Congress of Berlin and during the crisis of the Greek defeat by Turkey in 1897. Foreign Secretaries did not overlook the connections. Thus in 1886 Lord Rosebery had to override the Prince's protests at the imposition of a blockade of the Greek coast by an international fleet, when trouble was brewing in the Aegean. Family affinities, as well as his friendship with the Portuguese ambassador, Bertrand de Soveral, led to Edward's attempts to win British support in stabilising the regime of the King, Carlos I, his relation. However, he failed to secure a revision of the terms of the Anglo-Portuguese Colonial Convention, which proved highly unpopular in Portugal. The conduct of European policy was no longer simply a question of wishes of crowned heads, and the aspirations of royalty, at least in Britain, were increasingly limited to symbolic functions rather than interference in the serious business of foreign policy.

Meetings between heads of State were more likely to make than to heal breaches. Before visiting the young King of Spain, Alfonso XIII, shortly after the Carlists had been driven from Madrid, Edward had to give an assurance that he would 'in no way compromise His Majesty's Government'; and the contacts

'He should see what cards are in the hands of the players...'

59

between the Prince and the deposed French Imperial family (he offered shelter to the fleeing Emperor and Empress in 1871 and acted as pall-bearer at the funeral of the Prince Imperial in 1879; he also maintained a close friendship with the Orléanist Comte de Paris) were a cause for worry in the Cabinet. In this case the relationship was balanced by the fact that Edward cultivated friendships with many republican politicians; and his frequent visits *en garçon* to Paris and his involvement in the Exhibition of 1879, brought him popularity among the French people.

The most important and the most difficult personal relationship was with the German Emperor. The death of Frederick III, after his ninety-nine days' reign in 1888, was a family tragedy and a serious diplomatic event. It brought to the throne Victoria's favourite grandchild, but a nephew whom Edward found peculiarly repellent. They had quarrelled before because Edward had supported the love affair between the German Princess Victoria and the Crown Prince of Bulgaria – a union that had been strongly opposed both by the then Kaiser, William I, and by the future Kaiser, William II. A further source of tension was Edward's rather tactless remark to Herbert Bismarck, that, had Frederick lived, he might have begun the revision of Germany's position in Alsace-Lorraine, and might have returned the confiscated property of the King of Hanover. Such interference in domestic affairs led William to make a public rebuke, which was followed by the refusal to allow Edward to attend the Austrian army manoeuvres. Uncle and nephew were contrasting and jarring personalities; the one hedonistic, but controlled and diplomatic, the other flamboyant, arrogantly conscious of himself as supreme representative of the German nation. The Kaiser always remained jealous of the status of the British royal family, but did not hesitate to pour scorn on the easy-going affability of his uncle. Edward, in contrast, soon decided that 'William is a bully and most bullies, when tackled, are cowards'. The Prince found it hard to keep up the mask of cordial host when entertaining William at Cowes, whither the Kaiser came regularly with the aim of improving Anglo-German relations but usually with the result of damaging them. He was continually irritated by William's often successful efforts to prove that German yachts were superior to his own, and he was horrified at the speech made by William in 1895, in

which he spoke in bellicose terms of German-French relations.

In public the Prince could control his feelings – he even tried to soothe the Kaiser's feelings by granting him a position as colonel in the British army in 1884 – but dislike of the Kaiser's manner and of his interference in the early stages of the Boer War was given full rein in his private correspondence. This antipathy might have been unimportant, since the appeals of ministers could always persuade Edward to preserve outward good relations, but, as the diplomatic interests of Germany and Britain became more and more opposed, the conflict was heightened by the mutual distrust of the two men. Long before 1901 Edward was regarded in Germany 'as a votary of Parisian gaiety' and Edward was upset by the fact that his nephew took no action to restrain the insults in the German press after the Tranby Croft case (one cartoon showed the motto of the Prince of Wales transformed from 'Ich Dien' to 'I deal'). German diplomatists, of lesser calibre than Bismarck, regarded

Edward made frequent visits to France as Prince of Wales, and became involved in the Exhibition held in Paris in 1879. This photograph shows the exhibition viewed from beneath the Eiffel Tower.

61

PREVIOUS PAGES By 1887, Victoria's large family had so proliferated that she had become 'Grandmother of Europe', and Edward the 'Uncle of Europe'. This group by L. Tuxen, painted in the year of Victoria's Golden Jubilee, shows the Queen surrounded by her vast family. Edward stands behind her, dressed in black.

as ominous the Prince's efforts to avoid a crisis with the French in Indo-China in 1894, and were worried by the continuing link between the British and Russian royal families. Perhaps the influence of the Kaiser led to a tendency to exaggerate the powers of royalty, but the myth was itself a factor, and suspicions of the Prince's feelings towards Germany were widespread, long before his accession.

Whatever his views of European diplomacy, Edward had always given his support to Britain's imperial ventures. He had backed Britain's involvement in Egypt, and as early as 1869 had seen how vital a strategic interest the Suez Canal would become.

This cartoon from *Punch* alludes to Edward's acceptance in 1878 of the presidency of the British Commission of the Paris Exhibition. The figure on the right is Marshal McMahon, the president of the French Republic.

Imperial consideration took pride of place even above his desire for friendship with France, and during Kitchener's expedition to the Sudan in 1898 he wrote, 'The French are mad with rage, but ... it is useless paying any attention to their abuse'. In the late 1870s and 1880s he favoured the policies of Sir Bartle Frere in South Africa, and during the 1890s he faced with equanimity the prospect of another clash with the Boers. In 1897, after the failure of the Jameson Raid, he chided Lord Salisbury on his reluctance to meet Cecil Rhodes. Consequently, he was prepared to accept the isolation to which Britain found herself subject after the outbreak of the Boer War in 1899. He cancelled his annual visit to the Riviera and was conspicuously absent from the Paris International Exhibition in 1900.

These were symptoms of Britain's isolated position in the world. The tension between Britain and France, exacerbated by the Fashoda affair and reciprocated in the horror of the British royal family at the course of the Dreyfus case, extended far beyond quarrels in Africa. Britain lacked friends. Shortly after his accession, Edward tried to mollify the Czar in a letter that would perhaps have been impossible to convey through any but royal channels, in which he compared the South African situation with a hypothetical attack on Russia from Finland, made with Swedish support. So great was the hostility felt in Europe during this time that the very act of travelling on the Continent became dangerous. On 4 April 1900 Edward narrowly escaped assassination by a young anarchist, whilst at the Gare du Nord, Brussels, on his way to Denmark. The belief that Belgian treatment of the youth was too lenient and that their efforts to extradite him from France, whence he had fled, were too tardy, led to a coolness between Edward and King Leopold – but this coolness had the support of British public opinion, horrified as it was already by the reports of the appalling atrocities committed in the Congo under Belgian rule. Insular reaction and European mistrust confronted each other across the Channel. The Boer War was going badly and Britain was being humiliated. The Kaiser was, apparently, plotting a Continental union. Edward's accession in 1901 coincided with the nadir of Britain's standing in Europe and at the same time afforded him the opportunity to restore, through his own particular gifts, the harmony that had been lost.

3
The
Leader
of
Society
1861-1901

THE FINE HAND of diplomacy was not the aspect of the Prince of Wales's life best known to the British public. Nor did his chief interests lie in the more serious fields of home policy. But while it is hard to give him more than marginal credit for influence in affairs of State, he undoubtedly played a part in determining the pattern of behaviour in nineteenth-century upper-class society. To his contemporaries the Prince was seen, not as his mother wished, as an apprentice Prince Consort, but rather as the Prince Hal of his generation, an amateur of the full life, the epitome of all that glittered on the London scene. His creation was the society described by Clermont-Tonnere as 'A race of Gods and Goddesses descended from Olympus upon England', living 'upon a golden cloud, spending their riches as indolently and naturally as the leaves grown green'.

The picture was, of course, far from accurate and such adulation far from universal. The life of the Prince of Wales was largely a product of boredom and the pleasures derived from it were modified as he grew older and as he ran into periodic scandals and personal difficulties. Edward's activities did not mould a new high society, but they simply bestowed the patronage of royalty on the fringe of the aristocracy that had scarcely bowed to the middle-class ethic of morality and which looked for traditions to the eighteenth-century style of 'fast' living. Edward himself was no *roué* and the scandals with which he was associated were given inflated importance, because of the contrast with his father's mode of life, and because of the publicity given them by an expanding and often scandal-hungry press. Indeed the Prince might have regarded his behaviour as part of the royal tradition. Had not Bagehot declared that the role of the heir apparent was to taste 'all the world and the glory of it, whatever is most attractive, whatever is most seductive'? Yet even this was idealistic. What Edward did was to attach to himself a group of those whose company he found congenial, whose activities were the best antidote to the restrictions of his childhood and the boredom of forty-odd years of maturity, before he succeeded to the throne. His social sovereignty was never absolute – traditions among the upper classes remained diverse, ranging from the 'fast' companions of the Marlborough House set to the intellectual coterie of the 'Souls', and the moral rectitude of the 'Lambeth Penitents'.

PREVIOUS PAGES In 1896, Edward won his first Derby with his horse Persimmon. His victory was enormously popular, and the crowds gave him a tumultuous welcome when he led in Persimmon after the race.

Released from direct financial dependence on his parents, the Prince turned Marlborough House into a centre of London society and became a devotee of the clubs and of 'baccy' (baccarat) parties that went on late into the night. That the Prince should attend the music hall, that he should travel about London in a hansom cab, that he should be seen regularly in gambling clubs and at race meetings, all appeared to Victoria to be a grave affront to decency. 'What will become of the poor country when I die?', she wrote. 'If Bertie succeeds he would … spend his life in one whirl of amusements.' Her reaction is hardly surprising, given her constant belief that there was only one way for the image of monarchy to gain credit and that to depart from Albert's example was to invite disaster. In 1869 she complained to Edward: 'There is a *very* strong feeling against the luxuriousness and frivolity of society – and everyone comments on *my* simplicity.'

'*If you ever become King, you will find all these friends* most *inconvenient*'

Victoria never succeeded in exorcising her fear of the overthrow of the Crown and she was prone to make comparison between her son's acquaintances and the aristocracy in France 'just before the Revolution'. The Prince's choice of friends was inexplicable to her – in 1869 she voiced her objection to the Duke of Sutherland and Sir Samuel Baker meeting Edward in Egypt and strove to prevent Lord Charles Beresford and Lord Carrington accompanying him to India in 1875. Who were these men but the 'independent, haughty, fault-finding, fashionable set which was most inimical to the Prince Consort and herself'? Her son's accolade only encouraged those whom Albert had regarded as worthless philistines, whose activities dragged aristocracy into disrespect and threatened the institution of monarchy. Edward's constant appearance in public places destroyed the mystique of royalty. When the Queen drove in the park, people *noticed*. Victoria had restricted the royal circle to a select few, but here was the Prince in the company of freemasons, Jews, actresses and decadent aristocrats. 'If you ever become King', she wrote to him, 'you will find all these friends *most* inconvenient.' The 'ever' is significant. More than the moral effects on her son of such company, she feared for the future of the monarchy itself.

At first the Prince took for granted the double standard of Victorian society and deplored those who were found out in

Town and Country life

During the last part of the nineteenth century, urban life, especially in London, was rapidly changing for all levels of society. In the country, however, traditional customs were continued, marking the changing seasons of the year.

RIGHT A country cricket match in Sussex – rural life as yet untroubled by the development of industry and urbanisation. A painting by John Reid.

RIGHT St Giles Fair in Oxford in 1885. This fair dates back to the Middle Ages and takes place annually in the wide thoroughfare of St Giles during the students' summer vacation.

ABOVE In strong contrast, a street scene in London of the same period, showing the effects of industrialisation upon the city. Fleet Street is packed with buses, carriages and sheep being driven to market. Above, a train leaves Blackfriars Station – the railway was to open up the whole of Britain to the effects of the Industrial Revolution.

the scandals of the 1860s, the 'sad affairs' as he called them, which betrayed the aristocracy into 'washing dirty linen in public'. For all Prince Albert's efforts to impose a more salutary code, however, the wild element remained. The Marquis of Waterford eloped with the wife of his friend, and the heir to Lord Winchlow died in a brothel. Lord William d'Eresby, Joint Hereditary Grand Chamberlain of England, fleeced his mistress of thousands of pounds and then eloped with her maid. There was the revelation that Lord Euston had not only married a woman of low social position, but that she had turned out to be a bigamist. The activities of Henry Chaplin, son of the railway millionaire, and Lord Hastings, their personal rivalry for the affections of Lady Florence Paget, the 'Pocket Venus', and the financial ruin of Hastings in the 1868 Derby, followed by his early death, led *The Times* to comment: 'When a peer of high rank drags his dignity in the dirt ... he stains his order.'

Speculation ranged widely and an avid press fed on the tit-bits of the gossips. The Prince himself was rumoured to be associated with the actress Hortense Schneider, and the public was regaled with accounts of orgies in the Café Anglais during his visits to Paris, visits from which his wife was absent. Talk of gambling debts, and the presence of the Prince of Wales when a stag was killed in the goods yard at Paddington Station after a chase through the streets of London, indicated that the austere royalty of the 1840s and 1850s was not the only possible variety. In defence of his behaviour to his mother, Edward maintained that the aristocracy was still the backbone of England and was in no particular danger. They were performing such vital functions, he thought, as county magistrates and Lords Lieutenant and therefore 'some pleasure cannot be denied to them'. The argument was scarcely copper-bottomed: one should remember that Queen Victoria had had experience of the years before 1848 and her son had not. But Edward was on firmer ground in maintaining that withdrawal from the public gaze could be just as detrimental to the popularity of the monarchy. Here was more than fashionable revolt against parental strictness: Edward could reasonably argue that he was cultivating a section of British society whose former support was in danger of total alienation from the Crown during the period of Victoria and Albert.

In 1871, however, the Prince felt for the first time exposure to scandal. What had remained largely a matter between the Queen and her son was thrown open to the public view when Sir Charles Mordaunt filed a petition of divorce against his twenty-one year-old wife, citing two of the Prince's companions, Lord Cole and Sir Frederick Johnstone, as co-respondents. Mordaunt's wife, in a paroxysm of guilt caused by the blindness of one of her children, confessed that Sir Charles was not the father, and that she had 'done wrong' with 'the Prince of Wales and others, often and in open day'. The Prince was served with a *subpœna*, and although William Knollys had reason to know that the judge would prevent the Prince from coming under too heavy an attack, both the Prince and the Lord Chancellor feared that his reputation would suffer. Edward went into the witness box on 23 February and underwent a seven-minute examination by Sir Charles's counsel. He denied any suggestion of adultery and no cross-examination followed. At the end, according to *The Times*, 'there was a burst of applause'. It emerged from his own testimony and the evidence given by Lady Mordaunt's servants that he had been in the habit of calling on her during the afternoons, when her husband was absent at the House of Commons, and that during these visits he had often been left alone and undisturbed with her. His letters to Lady Mordaunt were printed in the provincial newspapers and also by *The Times* and, although they were pronounced 'simple, gossiping, everyday letters', he had evidently acted unwisely.

'Simple, gossiping, everyday letters'

The upshot was that Sir Charles's suit was rejected, the court finding for the counter-petition that Lady Mordaunt had been deranged when she made her confession (although some years later Sir Charles was granted his divorce on another petition, citing Lord Cole as the father of his child). The Queen defended her son throughout the crisis, wrote him understanding letters and urged on her ministers the necessity of defending him from attack. Nevertheless, she supported the Lord Chancellor in pointing out to Edward that, while 'so long as the nation has confidence in the personal character of the sovereign, the throne of this empire may be regarded as secure', his behaviour was causing doubts about the future. The hint of adultery by a member of the royal family came badly during the republican crisis, and less savoury aspects of the Prince's own life were frequently bandied about by the press. The *Sheffield Daily Telegraph* went too far, however, when it reported that the Prince was to be cited as co-respondent in a divorce case between Lord and Lady Sefton, and it was condemned of libel at Leeds Assizes in August 1871.

The agitation of this period, coupled with his illness, might have been expected to restrict Edward's social activities during the next few years. In fact, his life altered little and a glance at the list of companions he chose to take with him on his Indian tour in 1875–6 reveals that he still preferred the company of the 'bucks'. As he spent more time abroad, especially in France, he mixed with a wide circle containing both republican politicians and royalist aristocracy. The Prince sincerely loved Paris and the Riviera, and high society in the Third Republic responded by adopting fashions directly from 'le Prince de Galles'. By the turn of the century, the *gratins* were thoroughly anglophile. The Greffulhes and Breteuils were intimates of the Prince of Wales, *le betting* was to be enjoyed at Longchamps and unwanted members were *black boulé* at the Jockey Club. Whether in France or at home, the Prince's activities were innocent enough: a large part of the Indian tour was spent in big-game hunting and in the playing of practical jokes upon various members of the party. Practical joking seems to have represented the 'fast life' during this period and a country-house weekend was considered wild if pieces of soap were mixed with the cheese, or a cockerel was placed in the bedroom of a sleeping guest. Edward's appetite for such displays was almost limitless, but the victims of the rather twisted sense of humour were usually those who had similar tastes, and a rigid formality was maintained by him on all public occasions.

True, there were more serious lapses. In 1873 Francis Knollys wrote to Lord Rosebery asking him to place his London house at the disposal of the Prince for entertaining his 'actress friends' – but the rendezvous was intended as much for the use of the Prince's brother, the Duke of Edinburgh. The request was refused, but others may have been more accommodating. To most observers, the Prince seemed surrounded by 'a flotilla of white swans, their long necks supporting delicate jewelled heads' and the *demi-mondaines* were quick to claim the friendship if not more, of the heir apparent. Edward's name was linked with those of Sarah Bernhardt, Miss Chamberlayne (the daughter of an American millionaire), Lillie Langtry, Lady Brooke (later Lady Warwick), the Hon. Mrs George Keppel and Mrs Agnes Keyser. Some were evidently mistresses, others merely inamorata or companions. The Prince's penchant for beautiful women did not go unnoticed – 'he preferred men to books, and women to either'. The 'professional beauties' of the 1880s, women like Mrs Cornwallis-West, Mrs Luke Wheeler and Mrs Edward Langtry herself, were among the Prince's circle and were catalogued by the press for eager readership.

One of Edward's favourite ladies, Lillie Langtry, the 'Jersey Lily'.

LEFT Frances, Countess of Warwick, in fancy dress as the Queen of Assyria. She was Edward's mistress for some years, until she was converted to Socialism and fell out of favour.

RIGHT Sarah Bernhardt, the celebrated actress, also had her name linked with that of the Prince of Wales.

Yet a certain looseness among the upper echelons of society was quite permissible. Had not Gladstone himself declared that most of the Prime Ministers he had known had had mistresses, or even adulterous relationships? The affair between Lord Hartington and the Duchess of Manchester (with an interlude during Hartington's liaison with Catherine Walters, the famous 'Skittles') was an open secret, and did little damage to his career. There was no question of the royal mistresses exercising untoward influence on the Prince of Wales. When Lady Warwick

The famous Catherine Walters, or 'Skittles', who had affairs with many of Edward's friends.

OPPOSITE 'La Goulue', the dancer at the Moulin-Rouge celebrated in posters by Toulouse-Lautrec. Stories of her relationship with Edward circulated around dinner parties of the time.

turned to Socialism after a conversation with Robert Blatchford, she fell rapidly out of Edward's affections, and the often valuable work of Mrs Keppel in bringing the views of the Foreign Office to the King's notice was handled with discretion. Victoria herself consented to meet Lillie Langtry, the 'Jersey Lily', during her period in the royal favour, and Princess Alexandra accepted her husband's activities without loud complaint. What caused more concern were the occasions when the Prince was rumoured to be involved with women of a lower class and there was consternation when Count Deym, the Austrian ambassador, recounted at a dinner party the story that Edward had been greeted by the Moulin-Rouge dancer, La Goulue, with ''Ullo, Wales, est-ce que tu vas payer mon champagne?', and worse, that the Prince *had* paid for it! The nature of Edward's activities during his absences in France was not always clear, but there were certainly some omissions in his account to his mother: 'I like Cannes ... for its climate and society ... with regard to London ... the time we spend there is not *all* amusing ... to Homburg I go only for my health.' Yet Lady Warwick has provided an account of the trip to Paris in 1889, noting nothing more depraved than visits to the theatre and the Palais Royale, and dinner parties in the company of actresses like Bernhardt and Réjane, lunches with Messieurs

Eiffel and Edison, and shopping expeditions to the fashionable French stores. In all accounts there is no trace of seedy debauchery. A *boulevardier* Edward might be, an open exponent of degeneracy he certainly was not.

As a social leader, the Prince could find himself in trouble when scandal hit his friends. During the Indian tour, news reached his friend Lord Aylesford that his wife had eloped with another friend of the Prince, the notorious 'Sporting Joe' – Lord Blandford, who had left his own wife to go and live with Lady Aylesford. The Prince, upset at being deprived of Aylesford's company, condemned Blandford out of hand. The affair brought about a quarrel between Edward and Lord Randolph Churchill (Blandford's brother) who tried to persuade the Prince to discourage Aylesford from divorcing his wife. Churchill showed Princess Alexandra some letters from the Prince to Lady Aylesford which showed Edward's attitude to be somewhat hypocritical. On hearing of this, Edward, who had only reached Egypt, despatched Lord Charles Beresford to challenge Lord Randolph to a duel – an offer which Churchill naturally refused. Edward was determined to pursue him, but the Government was clearly more sensitive to the likely effects if Churchill produced the letters in a divorce suit. Lord Hardwicke, the Lord Chancellor, began a discreet negotiation and shortly after the Prince returned, Aylesford agreed not to proceed with his divorce. Whatever the rights and wrongs of the case, the Prince was furious at Churchill's part in the affair and demanded written apology, from both him and the Marlborough family. These were forthcoming, but Edward refused to be seen in Lord Randolph's company for eight years thereafter, and the social life of the Churchills suffered greatly.

The hint of scandal was never far from the Prince's companions. In 1883 Lady Blandford went to the courts to obtain a decree of separation from her husband, and in 1885 Sir Charles Dilke, by now a close friend of the Prince, was cited as co-respondent in the Crawford divorce case. Valentine Baker of the 10th Hussars was found guilty of indecent assault, and in 1889 the Prince heard that Lord Arthur Somerset (Podge as he was known to his friends, the Prince included) had been discovered in a homosexual brothel during a police raid. The latter incident was hushed up to Edward's satisfaction and the 'unfortunate

'The time we spend there is not all amusing'

lunatic' was allowed to flee the country. There was also a good deal of hushing-up regarding the activities of Edward's own son, Albert Victor, whose debauchery became a serious worry to his parents. Then in 1891 Edward found himself again in a public court.

During September 1890 he had stayed at Tranby Croft, the house of Arthur Wilson, a shipowner, for the St Leger race meeting. The evenings were given over to the popular but illegal game of baccarat and Wilson's son noticed one of the players, Sir William Gordon-Cumming, indulging in *la pousette* – a device which enabled the player to vary the size of his stake after he had seen the cards held by himself and the bank. In two evenings Sir William had won £225 using this underhand manoeuvre. He had been observed by five witnesses, however, and on 10 September he was charged with cheating by Lord Coventry and Colonel Owen Williams. Cumming sought the advice of the Prince of Wales but was told that there was no use denying the charge. He agreed to sign a pledge never to play cards again, a pledge that bound all the signatories to silence. To this document, along with the five witnesses and the other players, the Prince put his name. Unfortunately, renewed rumours of Sir William's conduct broke out in 1891 and he felt obliged to bring his accusers to court in an attempt to clear his name.

The Prince and Francis Knollys did everything to hinder his efforts and tried unsuccessfully to have Cumming brought before an army inquiry or an inquiry held by the Guards Club Committee. As in the Mordaunt case, Queen Victoria gave support to her son, condemning those who had asked him to sign the document and asking only for a pledge that he would never play baccarat again. Another appearance in court was inevitable. Cumming's solicitor, convinced of his client's innocence, refused to forego a cross-examination. The case against the Prince was based on his encouragement of an illegal game and his disregard of Article 42 of Queen's Regulations, which laid down that dishonourable conduct by an officer, if witnessed by a fellow officer (and was not Edward a high ranking officer in the army?) must be reported to the offender's commanding officer. The Prince attended court regularly from 1 to 9 June, and during his own testimony

TRANBY CROFT,
SEP. 11, 1890.

1. GEN. O. WILLIAMS.
2. LORD COVENTRY.
3. LYCETT GREEN.
4. BERKELEY LEVETT.
5. MRS LYCETT GREEN.
6. LORD A. SOMERSET.
7. REUBEN SASSOON.
8. LORD E. SOMERSET.
9. STANLEY WILSON.
10. TYRWHITT WILSON (EQUERRY)

11. ARTHUR WILSON.
12. CHRISTOPHER SYKES.
13. COUNT LUDSKEW.
14. MISS NAYLOR.
15. MRS. GEN. O. WILLIAMS.
16. MRS. A. WILSON.
17. LIEUT. COL. SIR C. GORDON CUMMING.
18. H.R.H.
19. COUNTESS COVENTRY.
20. LADY BROUGHAM.

declared his confidence in those who had claimed to see Sir William cheating. After that the result was never really in doubt and the verdict was given in favour of the defendants. Gordon-Cumming was promptly expelled from the army, his clubs and society in general. The Prince was left ruefully contrasting the apparent inability of the Government to protect him with its shielding of him in 1871, and he was not pleased when Lord Stanhope, Secretary-of-State for War, had to apologise on his behalf to the House of Commons for not reporting Cumming's activities under Article 42.

The reactions to the affair were predictably similar to what had happened before. Victoria once again (with the support of the Lord Chancellor) urged him to promise to reform his mode of life and to write a public letter to the Archbishop of Canterbury proclaiming his dislike of gambling, and swearing never to play baccarat again. Radicals made play with the likelihood that the recent grant of £36,000 to Edward's children might simply be swallowed up in gambling debts. Nonconformist clamour against the moral evils of such pursuits were loud. W. T. Stead wrote of the 'Prayer Gauge' by which he calculated the number of prayers said in churches for the Prince and declared their result to be a gambling scandal, and the Scottish Free Church went so far as to remove Edward's name from their prayers altogether. The 'Lambeth Penitents', a group of high-born ladies, including the Duchess of Leeds, Lady Tavistock, Lady Aberdeen, Lady Zetland and Lady Stanhope, appealed to the Princess of Wales to attend their services, aimed at promoting the moral welfare of society. The Princess, with Victoria's support, refused to join. Edward was equally robust. Despite the warnings of *The Times* and the somewhat disingenuous horror of the Kaiser at his behaviour, he refused to issue a public repudiation of his sporting activities. After conversations with the Archbishop, he wrote him a private letter in which he distinguished between gambling, of which he disapproved, and betting, which he maintained was harmless. He pointed out that his first experience of playing cards for money had been at the house of Bishop Wilberforce at Oxford in the 1860s, and claimed that horse racing was a sport followed eagerly by a large section of the British public. Later, the new vogue for bridge allowed Edward to cut down on

OPPOSITE The house party at Tranby Croft, September 1890 – the setting for the notorious gaming scandal which involved the Prince of Wales. The host was Arthur Wilson (11) the shipowner, and the guest caught cheating at baccarat was Sir William Gordon-Cumming (17).

The Prince's circle

Edward's choice of friends was frequently criticised by certain sections of high society – in particular they complained of the influx of wealthy Jews into the royal circle.

RIGHT Lord Nathan Rothschild.
BELOW Sir Ernest Cassel (left) and Baron Hirsch. These men were to help Edward with their financial acumen – Hirsch helped to begin work on the Berlin to Baghdad Railway, while Ernest Cassel aided the finance of the Aswan Dam.

Spy's drawing of Sir Thomas Lipton, the grocer millionaire friend of Edward. He was a very keen yachtsman, and Edward spent much time on his yachts.

baccarat; but Sir Frederick Ponsonby recounts an instance, as late as 1907, when baccarat was played in his presence, apparently at the Queen's request, although the King did not take part. Edward refused to give hypocritical encouragement to the puritans and Tranby Croft in no way undermined his enthusiasm for country-house parties – although Tranby Croft itself was not visited again.

In the same year, 1891, Edward found himself involved in a personal conflict similar to the Aylesford divorce scandal of 1871. Lord Charles Beresford had returned to the service of the navy and to his wife in 1889, courses which his mistress, Lady Brooke, considered foolish. Foolishly too she put this view on paper and the letter fell into Lady Beresford's hands. Lady Brooke then turned to the Prince and begged him to get it returned to her or destroyed. Edward, very much under the influence of her beauty, persuaded Lady Beresford's solicitor to agree. Lady Beresford herself was more reticent and sent the letter to her relatives, the Waterfords, refusing either to destroy or to return it. Lord Charles, who disapproved strongly of the Prince's interference in his affairs, went off to join his squadron in the Mediterranean, but his wife, left in London, experienced social ostracism by the Prince of Wales and his court. So intolerable was this that by 1891 she had put up the house for sale, and was prepared to leave for the country. Hearing of this, Beresford became wildly angry. He had been an intimate friend of Edward for thirty years and he now threatened to reveal to the press what he knew of the Prince's private life. Lady Beresford's claim that 'several people wanted to make use of the story at the next general election' may not have been realistic as a threat to Lord Salisbury's Government, but the Cabinet remained sensitive to the thought of another exposure so soon after Tranby Croft. Salisbury intervened; Beresford was prevented from making his statement. The price was the Beresfords' reintroduction to court and Lady Brooke's temporary exclusion. Edward never forgave Beresford for his attempt to blackmail his future sovereign and although the letter was eventually returned to Lady Brooke, the affair left deep scars – it was influential in Edward's strong support for Sir John Fisher against Beresford in the struggle within the Admiralty in 1909.

These troubles were, however, the last which really

threatened the Prince of Wales's future. He shared in the general increase in popularity of the monarchy which swelled with the Jubilees of 1887 and 1897. The public was becoming used to his activities, just as it sympathised with his position as an ageing Prince waiting patiently for his inheritance. The *fin de siècle* assault on the Victorian ethic, whilst still confined largely to the intellectual élite, took some of the sting from the reproaches of the 'nonconformist conscience'. Thus, Lord Randolph Churchill's earlier threat that exposure of Edward's private life might prevent his succession to the throne, had become virtually meaningless by the 1890s. Edward's style was less alien to the public than it had been during the austere years of the mid-century and his role was now valuable in so far as it 'afforded vicarious enjoyment to the millions and social opportunities to millionaires'. The Prince continued to enjoy club society (in the 1860s he had been responsible for the establishment of the Marlborough Club, because White's had refused to allow smoking in the morning room; in 1895 he resigned from the Travellers' Club after Cecil Rhodes was black-balled). His habits of dress – he thought little of changing clothes six times a day – set the fashion for the smart set, and among his innovations were the black Homburg hat, the dinner jacket, shorter tails on evening wear, and the wearing of tweeds at race meetings; more slavish imitators adopted his style of handshake and the design of his horses' harness.

'Several people wanted to make use of the story'

Complaints about his choice of companions were still voiced by certain sections of the upper class, who were outraged when Edward entertained the notorious rake, the Prince of Orange, at Sandringham and were horrified at the influx of wealthy Jews into the royal circle. That the Prince should entertain the Rothschilds, Baron Hirsch, Sir Ernest Cassel, Louis Bischoffsheim, the Sassoons, Sir Blundell Maple and Sir Thomas Lipton, Colonel W. W. Astor and the South African millionaire J. B. Robinson, was bad enough – that he should consent to visit and stay at their homes was terrible. Even *The Times* objected to his hob-nobbing with 'American cattle-men and prize-fighters'. But the Prince refused to give up the company of those whose hospitality he enjoyed and whose financial acumen was essential to one dependent, as he was, on an income that without shrewd investment would never have enabled him to live the life he desired. When he wished to sell the racing yacht *Britannia*, Edward was not prepared to quibble that the potential buyer had made his money out of the promotion of Bovril. Wealth, rather than pedigree, provided the key to good company, and the cosmopolitan Prince, who as a young man had bathed in the glitter of the *parvenu* aristocracy of Imperial France, spurned the more discriminatory voices of the European and British courts. In this he was perhaps a man more of the twentieth century than his detractors. Viennese society was shocked when Edward stayed at the house of the Jewish Baron Hirsch, and Victoria refused to allow Hirsch to attend a state concert in London in 1890. Yet Hirsch was one of the great promoters whose work began the Berlin-Baghdad railway; and Ernest Cassel helped to finance the Aswan Dam. For good or ill, the future King was on the side of progress.

In spite of all the follies and extravagance of his social circle, Edward also stood for a solid attachment to his family, not at all typical of the 'late Victorian revolt' with which his name is sometimes associated. An article in *The Times* in 1888 referred to his contribution to 'the great religion of the family' – an assessment which might seem hard to reconcile with the image of the Prince as an out-and-out rake. For all his waywardness, there was never much doubt that his mother would stand by him. He showed scarcely any resentment against his parents for the rigours of his youth. On the death of his brother-in-law, Frederick of Germany, he wrote to Victoria: 'I felt ... I had parted from the noblest and best man I had ever known, except for my ever-to-be-lamented father'; and, although he might disagree with his mother over policy and object to her preference in trusting his brother Leopold with confidential information, he respected her as both mother and Queen. Edward was always conscious of himself as a member of the royal caste and never wavered in his insistence on correct behaviour on formal occasions. In 1887 he wrote that 'refinement of feeling in the younger generation does not exist', and told another correspondent, 'The age of chivalry has, alas, passed ... both in social and political life'. In private he might complain about the Queen's obstinacy, or the personal shortcomings of Czar Nicholas II, but in public his behaviour towards royalty was impeccable. Thus he provided King

'If he were a cowboy, I would love him just the same'

Kalakua of the Sandwich Islands with magnificent entertainment during his visit to England in 1881, dismissing objections with the comment: 'Either the brute is a King, or he is a common or garden nigger; and if the latter, what's he doing here?' He was friendly to such minor royalty as Milan of Serbia, whom he met during a visit to Russia, and when the representative of the Obrenovich dynasty was assassinated in June 1903, he refused to have anything to do with his successor, the Karageorgevich King Peter, until all the regicide officers had been retired from the Serbian army.

Edward was undoubtedly fortunate in his wife. Alexandra's interests lay primarily with her children and her family, but she was prepared to put up with Edward's affairs in a manner which shows either great naïvety or great tolerance. She was genuinely attached to her husband. 'You may think I like marrying Bertie for his position', she wrote to Princess Victoria of Prussia, 'but if he were a cowboy, I would love him just the same'. She displayed exceptional diplomacy and discretion in dealing with Victoria's doubts about the marriage. ('It is no small compliment to the Princess to say that her personal qualities are thought sufficient to outweigh the dislike that is felt to many of her connections', Arthur Paget had noted.) Perhaps she was also conscious of the great honour that had come to her on being raised from the poor Danish family to one of the highest positions of European royalty. To state, that 'like many other great ladies of the day … she looked upon her husband's indiscretions as proof of his abounding manhood' is probably to exaggerate, but Alexandra seems not to have complained, and indeed was able to jest at Miss Chamberlayne, whom she referred to as 'Chamberpots', when she was entertained at Sandringham; she even came to enjoy the company of Mrs Keppel. Her own beauty and grace survived the years and compensated somewhat for the deafness which cut her off at court. Her charitable work won her much public affection and the devoted, if platonic, love of the Prince's equerry, Oliver Montagu. Edward was ready to defend her against Victoria's occasional displeasure. 'None of us is perfect . . . but she is certainly not selfish and her whole life is wrapped up in her children', he wrote to his mother. For her sake, Edward was prepared to put up with the boring austerity of the Danish court, a burden he would not otherwise have tolerated. He always consulted her when public scandal threatened and she supported him in 1871 and 1875 – although when the troubles of 1891 mounted up, the Princess extended her tour of Denmark and Russia until the illness of Prince George called her back. Deafness and a limp, which was brought on by an attack of rheumatic fever in 1867, prevented her involvement in the hectic social round and she was content to be a good mother to her children, to follow her deep religious instincts and to devote her interest to the welfare of her own Danish family.

Victoria sometimes found fault with Alexandra and in a sense blamed her for Edward's shortcomings – 'I do not think she makes his home comfortable', she wrote in 1886. With the birth of her grandchildren, however, their relationship improved. Alexandra's first son, christened Albert Victor, was born prematurely on 8 January 1864 and was speedily followed by Prince George, Princess Louise, Princess Victoria and Princess Maud. The last child, Prince Alexander, was born in 1871, but lived only a few hours. Her daughters were devoted to their 'darling Motherdear' and she to them, to such an extent that fears were held for their prospects of marriage. Nevertheless, Princess Louise was married to the Duke of Fife in 1888, and in 1896 Princess Maud married Prince Charles of Denmark, the future King of Norway. Only Princess Victoria died a spinster, although during the 1890s there were rumours that Lord Rosebery had been a candidate for her hand.

Edward was constantly concerned with the education of his sons. Aware of the failings of his own education, he determined that they should avoid isolation. At first he considered sending Prince Albert Victor to Wellington College and Prince George into the Royal Navy, but their tutor, the Rev. J. Neale, was convinced that the elder brother needed the company of the younger and advised against any separation. Both were therefore sent as cadets to the training ship *Britannia* and thence on a series of cruises on HMS *Bacchante*. Serious problems arose, however, with the development of the eldest son, who displayed a weakness of mind which compared unfavourably with the more robust nature of Prince George. While the latter enjoyed his career in the navy, Albert Victor was unhappy both at Cambridge, where he attended Trinity College in 1883,

OPPOSITE On 8 January 1864, Princess Alexandra gave birth to her first child, Albert Victor, later Duke of Clarence.

90

The Grandmother of Europe

These family photographs show how close was Victoria's family, despite its enormous size.

The Russian royal family on one of their visits to Balmoral, 1896. Left to right: Czarina Alix, Grand Duchess Olga, Czar Nicholas II, Queen Victoria and the Prince of Wales.

Edward and his family on board the royal yacht *Osborne* in 1880. Left to right: Princesses Maud and Louise, Prince Albert Victor, Princess Alexandra, Prince George, and in front, Princess Victoria and the Prince of Wales.

ABOVE Edward and his family when they were grown up. Left to right: Albert Victor, the Duke of Clarence (soon to die of pneumonia), Princess Maud (then married to the King of Norway), Princess Alexandra, Princess Louise (then Duchess of Fife) and the Prince of Wales. In front, Prince George (later George v), Princess Victoria.

LEFT Prince George married Princess May of Teck and their first son, the Duke of Windsor (Edward VIII) was born in 1894. Here Victoria is seen with her son, grandson and great-grandson – four sovereigns of Great Britain.

ABOVE The royal house party at Ascot in 1896. In the centre are grouped from left to right: Prince Edward and Princess Alexandra, the Duke of Cambridge, Princess May of Teck and Prince George.

ABOVE RIGHT The Prince of Wales with his horse Persimmon, which won the Derby in 1896.

and in the army. After he had come of age he began to lead a dissolute life and his marriage proved difficult to arrange. Having rejected Princess Margaret of Germany, who was, in any case, not keen on the match, he was turned down by Alix of Hesse, who later became the last Czarina of Russia. Finally, he became involved in a profound love affair with Princess Hélène d'Orléans. Despite the fact that an engagement was announced in August 1890 and the arrangement was approved by Edward, Alexandra and the Princess's mother, the religious difficulties and the opposition of the Comte d'Orléans and the Pope, proved insuperable. The Government was relieved, for even though Hélène had offered to become Protestant, the shadow of anti-popery in Britain remained powerful. Eventually a marriage was arranged for Albert Victor, now Duke of Clarence, and shortly after his return from a tour of India he proposed to and was accepted by Princess May of Teck. But in the early months of 1892 the Duke was taken ill and died of pneumonia. Edward's sorrow was deep: 'To lose our eldest son', he wrote to Gladstone, 'is one of those calamities one can

95

never really get over ... though, as time goes on, our duties and occupation will have to be followed ... our daily life will remind me of the gap made amongst our children.' To his mother he wrote that he would 'gladly ... have given my life for him, as I put no value on mine'.

In the following year, however, Princess May was married to Prince George – a match for which precedent existed in the marriage of Dagmar, Alexandra's sister, to the future Czar Alexander III, after the death of her previous fiancé, Alexander's elder brother. No English heir apparent had become a grand-father during the life of the sovereign, until Princess Louise gave birth to a daughter in 1891. In the years before his accession, *l'art d'être grandpère* was increasingly in evidence in Edward's behaviour, as his son George became the father successively of the future Duke of Windsor (Edward VIII) in June 1894, Prince Albert (George VI) in 1895 and Prince Henry (the Duke of Gloucester) in 1900.

The sadnesses of his family occupied much of Edward's time. He lived through the death of two brothers, the Dukes of Albany and Edinburgh, and shortly before his accession he learnt that his sister, Vicky, the Dowager Empress of Germany, was dying of cancer. There had been fears for the life of Prince George in 1891 when he had contracted that scourge of Victoria's family, cholera. Many of the Prince's tours had been to attend the various funerals and marriages of his relations in Scandinavia and Greece, Russia and Germany, and these family connections helped him to form his understanding of Europe and his conception of foreign affairs. Family concerns impinged closely on domestic politics, too, in relation to the question of financial provision for the Prince's family. In spite of the work of Sir Dighton Probyn (who replaced Sir William Knollys as comptroller and treasurer of the Prince's household in 1877) and the financial advice offered by the Rothschilds and his millionaire friends, Edward's accounts were still under some strain. Efforts to obtain an advance for his eldest son had begun in 1882, but the Government was never happy in pressing such claims on the Commons. It was not until 1889 that Salisbury, relying on Gladstone's support, brought proposals for granting allowances to the Prince's children before the House. Opposition at once broke out among the more radical wing of the

OPPOSITE Princess Alexandra, a portrait by Sir Luke Fildes.

OPPOSITE Edward, with
his trophy of the shoot,
photographed in the
Highlands in 1893.

Liberal party, led by Sir William Harcourt and John Morley, supported by the more extreme radicals like Labouchère and Charles Bradlaugh. Gladstone, although able to bring the Irish Nationalists into line, had to keep the grant down to a minimum and take care to establish no precedent for the indiscriminate grant of Government money to the members of the younger generation. Finally, it was decided that instead of the generous individual allowances at first proposed, a quarterly payment should be made direct to the Prince of Wales of £36,000 a year out of which 'he would be empowered to make such assignments . . . to his children as HRH should think fit'.

Such restrictions on his finances did not mean that the Prince's natural penchant for sporting activities was strictly curbed. Although he had a reputation for the more sedentary aspects of the good life, addiction to cigars and cigarettes, and a love of rich food and good drink which became legendary, he was also interested in outdoor activities. 'The best plan to maintain health is, I am sure, to be careful of your diet,' he wrote, a trifle sardonically, in 1894, 'and take as much exercise as possible.' Racing was the most absorbing of his interests and one critic noted that he attended twenty-eight race meetings in 1890, nearly three times as many as he attended days in the House of Lords. He enjoyed equally the excitement of the race and the raffish camaraderie of racing society, though it was only relatively late in his career that he became an owner himself.

Shortly after his return from India, relying on the advice of Lord Marcus Beresford, who later became manager of the Royal Stud, Edward began to build up a stable that was the foundation of the royal family's continuing interest in racing. His most notable successes were three Derby winners (Persimmon in 1896, Diamond Jubilee in 1900 and Minoru in 1909) and a victory in the Grand National by Ambush II in 1900. On the whole the Prince's racing exploits won him both popularity and some financial success. He headed the list of winning owners in 1900 with £29,586, worth roughly £100,000 in today's values. The largest bet he ever placed on an individual horse to win, was £600 on Hirsch's Matchbox in the Grand Prix de Paris in 1894, a horse who was beaten by a neck. Unlike Lord Rosebery, whose successes were liable to be offset by the outrage of Liberal nonconformist supporters, the Prince

98

The three daughters of
Edward and Alexandra,
painted by S.P.Hall in
1893. They are, from left
to right: Princess Louise,
Princess Victoria and
Princess Maud.

was a national figure. Lord Grey recalled that news of the
victory of Persimmon in the Derby 'vibrated through' a community as far away as Bulawayo with a sense of 'thrilling
pleasure'. The Natural History Museum was pleased to accept
the skeleton of that famous horse, presented to it after his death
in 1908 – one wonders what Prince Albert would have thought!

The Prince also dabbled in other sports, tennis, golf, and
the more traditional aristocratic pursuits of fox-hunting and
shooting. Game shooting was one of Edward's greatest passions
and he was appreciative of a really good shooting party. Whole
hecatombs of birds were slaughtered on the aristocratic

preserves of Central Europe. In Britain, Sandringham provided regular pheasant and partridge shoots and at Abergeldie Castle deer-stalking was much enjoyed until the Prince grew too old and preferred to have the deer driven towards him. If an aspiring social climber wished to make the acquaintance of the Prince, he did well to buy an estate with a record of thousands of grouse killed, since such a lure was unlikely to be refused. There was also the Prince's passion for racing yachts. His first was purchased in 1876, and in the 1890s the cutter *Britannia*, built especially for him, brought him much success. Edward's interest stemmed from his early days on the Isle of Wight at Osborne and reached its peak during the last decade of the century, when he regularly presided at the Cowes Regatta. His successes inspired the emulation of Kaiser William II, who first visited Cowes in 1889, and regularly attended from 1891–5. When *Britannia* was seen to have the measure of the first of the Kaiser's entrants, *Meteor I*, William ordered the construction of *Meteor II*, which became the most successful yacht of the day. Faced with such dedicated opposition, the Prince's own interest declined.

All these activities filled the years as the Prince moved steadily through middle age. In 1900 he was fifty-nine. His apprenticeship, his period of waiting, had been a long one and there were some who now argued that his habits of mind, agreeable enough in a Prince of Wales, were not best suited to the demands of kingship. As the century closed, and Victoria's infirmities became more obvious, there was little doubt that his qualities would soon be put to the test as head of State. He was no longer the gay young buck of the 1860s; yet there would be a very different style of monarchy from the long decades of Victoria's withdrawal and her later years as imperial figure-head.

4 The Long-awaited

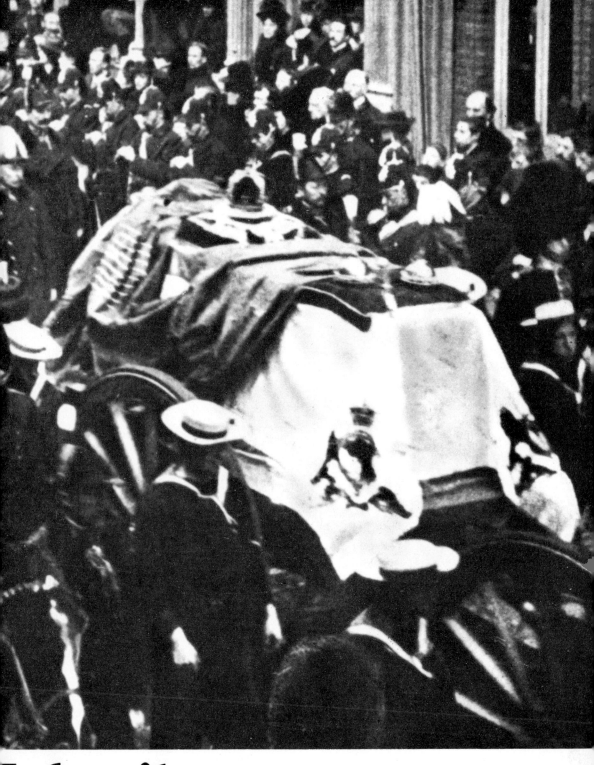

Inheritance 1901

Queen Victoria – one of the last photographs taken of her.

IN DECEMBER 1900 Queen Victoria went to Osborne for the last time. Rheumatism, eye disease and aphasia were signs that her strength was declining. She was nearly eighty-two and on 15 January 1901 she took her last drive in the grounds that Albert had laid out so many years before. The Prince of Wales was warned on 18 January of his mother's serious condition and after dining that evening with Agnes Keyser, he left the Highlands for Osborne. The Duke of Connaught was also *en route* and, mindful perhaps of the example of Edward, who had started at once for Russia on hearing of the illness of the late Czar Alexander III, the Kaiser arrived in London on the 20 January. Edward escorted him down to Osborne. By the next day Victoria was sinking fast. Around her bedside assembled her closest family, the attention of her grandson the Kaiser being constant and devoted. At 12.15 p.m. the Queen put out her arms and called, 'Bertie', and the Prince broke into sobs as he embraced his mother. It was Victoria's last conscious utterance. At 6.30 p.m. on Tuesday 22 January 1901, the Queen drew her last breath in the arms of the Kaiser. She had reigned for sixty-four years, longer than any other British sovereign, and had lived three days longer than George III. At last Edward came into his inheritance.

Leaving the Kaiser in charge of Osborne, Edward attended the Accession Council at St James's Palace, where he made a masterly extempore speech. After declaring that Albert was a name which should remain for ever reserved for 'Albert the Good', he chose the name of Edward for his own kingship; he talked of the 'irreparable loss' he and the country had suffered through Victoria's death and he promised wholeheartedly, 'My constant endeavour will be always devoted to walk in her footsteps … I am fully determined to be a constitutional sovereign, in the strictest sense of the word, to work for the good and amelioration of my people.' His new titles were to include that of Emperor of India and King of the United Kingdom of Great Britain and Ireland *and of the British Dominions Overseas*, the last clause being an innovation.

PREVIOUS PAGES
Queen Victoria's funeral procession in 1901. Following the gun carriage are the Kaiser, Edward and the Duke of Connaught.

At Osborne the Queen's death brought unexpected problems of protocol because the last monarch had died as long ago as 1837. The Duke of Connaught discovered that the Queen's Company of the Grenadier Guards had the right to stand guard over the coffin and thus the 60th Rifles, who had already been summoned, had to be replaced. The guard was joined by one member of the household in rotation, a duty which Frederick Ponsonby found particularly trying, 'on account of the very strong scent of the tuberroses and gardenias'. Victoria had laid down instructions for the funeral three years earlier, but in the stunned atmosphere some of the details went awry. As the coffin was carried over to the mainland, Edward noticed that the flag in his boat, following the one bearing Queen Victoria's remains, was at half-mast, and pointed out, 'The King is alive'. At Windsor, the team of horses drawing the gun carriage on which the coffin was borne kicked over the traces and destroyed them – hence the expedient of hauling the carriage into London by a team of men from the naval guard of honour. Finally, during the rehearsal for the internment in the Frogmore Mausoleum, it was discovered that unless the coffin were reversed as it was taken off the carriage, the dead Queen would end up on the tomb the opposite way to the marble figure of Prince Albert. The household staff coped perfectly. London saw only a stately procession, graced by the Emperor of Germany, the Kings of Belgium, Portugal, Greece and a dozen other heads of State among those who followed the cortège. Lady Battersea voiced the general sense of tribulation: 'Words seem to express less than facts ... black mourning London; black mourning England; black mourning Empire. The sensation of universal change haunted me.'

Seldom can the British public have been so acutely aware that an era was ending. Biographies of the late Queen abounded: G. A. Henty's *Queen Victoria*, Mrs Gurney's *The Childhood of Queen Victoria*, F. Aitken's *Victoria, the Wellbeloved*, and Mrs O. F. Walters's *Pictures and Stories from Queen Victoria's Life*. On the level of sheer gossip came the more lurid *Private Life of Queen Victoria by One of Her Majesty's Servants*. Arthur Mee could offer *King and Empire, the Life History of Edward* VII and E. Spencer *The King's Racehorses. A History of the Connexion of His Majesty Edward* VII *with the National Sport*. It seemed to be a time of summing up, of unease rather than optimism; and as for the monarchy itself, the sense of loss outweighed the gains which were immediately felt. Many doubted the new King's ability: *The Times's* editorial on 23 January talked of the

Sir Dighton Probyn, who
became Edward's Keeper
of the Privy Purse.

Frederick Ponsonby,
assistant private secretary
to the new King.

'temptations' to which the Prince had been subject, and honestly enough commented: 'We cannot pretend that there is nothing in his long career which those of us who respect and admire him could wish otherwise.' The language was cautious, but it covered obvious sentiment. In some nonconformist pulpits there were dire warnings drawn from the example of that perennial bogey, George IV.

Buckingham Palace, before alterations in 1911. On accession, Edward modernised and refitted it as his royal residence in London. Up to this period it had been treated rather like a museum in memory of Prince Albert.

But Edward was no stripling to absorb moral tracts. As Lord Salisbury pointed out in the House of Lords, he 'has been familiar with our political and social life for more than one generation and he enjoys a universal and enormous popularity … he is loved in foreign countries and in foreign courts'. He had a record of public service and his work for the London Hospitals Fund or the new Queen's long list of charities could arouse feelings of positive enthusiasm. Moreover, if Edward could never be, in the words of the ubiquitous Irishman, 'the King his Mother was', he might make up for his lack of symbolic 'weight' by a more up-to-date conception of the monarchy's function and purpose.

Whether spontaneously, or as a result of skilful publicity, the sense that the new King was more modern, more in touch with his times, was not long in developing. Edward's staff regarded

107

the old officers of the household as hopelessly old-fashioned, and he himself was not prepared to treat the past as a sacred trust which must be preserved. He determined to dispose of Osborne, whose architectural style and furnishing remained a monument to the taste of Victoria and Albert. Eventually (and not without a good deal of family hostility) the building was given over to naval cadets for use as a training centre and only the central rooms were preserved as a memorial to the late Queen. Buckingham Palace, for so long deserted, was modernised and prepared as the royal residence in London. The 'Sepulchre' of Albert's rooms was gutted and the whole palace was rearranged. The plumbing and the paintings were both replaced by more modern styles, and boxes of Victorian mementoes and a great deal of heavy furniture were carried off to be stored in Windsor Castle.

Out too went the gloom of the Victorian court. There were many innovations in court procedure that showed a new conception of monarchy was present. Dreary afternoon 'drawing-rooms' were replaced by evening courts held in the ballroom of Buckingham Palace. Clearly Edward was drawing on the experience he had gained from foreign courts to remodel his own. Indeed, at times these courts assumed a trifle too much levity – the playing of popular airs, which Edward liked, was not appreciated by Sir Walter Parratt, the Master of the King's Musick, nor by Frederick Ponsonby, who noted the incongruity of 'eminent men being knighted while comic songs were being played'.

While the glitter of the new court confirmed Edward's position at the apex of the London social pyramid, his love of ceremony was also appreciated by the public at large. The pageantry of the first State Opening of Parliament proved to be in marked contrast to the austerity of Victoria's infrequent public appearances. The King encouraged similar ostentation among the peers, who were instructed to arrive in their finest carriages, already robed. Edward resumed the practice of opening Parliament in person, for the first time since 1886, and read his speech from the throne himself. Thereafter, the numerous State visits and a series of royal progresses through the country gave the King a news value widely welcomed after the long withdrawal of his mother. For the first time, accounts

OPPOSITE Coronation postcards of 1902, showing Edward, Alexandra, Prince George and Princess May in their coronation robes.

108

Published by Stewart & Woolf, London, W.C. Series 105. Printed at the Fine Art Works in Prussia.

His Majesty King Edward VII.

Published by Stewart & Woolf, London, W.C. Series 105. Printed at the Fine Art Works in Prussia.

Her Majesty Queen Alexandra.

Published by Stewart & Woolf, London, W.C. Series 105. Printed at the Fine Art Works in Prussia.

H.R.H. the Prince of Wales.

Published by Stewart & Woolf, London, W.C. Series 105. Printed at the Fine Art Works in Prussia.

H.R.H. the Princess of Wales.

OPPOSITE Edward and
Alexandra attending their
first state opening of
Parliament, 14 February
1901, from a painting by
S. Begg.

of the sovereign's activities became a regular feature in the
popular newspapers. By 1908 Lord Northcliffe, the great
newspaper proprietor, could write that 'the King has become
such an immense personality in England that … the space
devoted to the movements of royalty has quintrupled since
His Majesty came to the throne'. Edward's style of life did not
perhaps *create* the phenomenon of which Sir Sidney Lee spoke
– that 'rapid evolution from the dullness and decorum of the
Victorian era to the more social brightness and vivacity of the
Edwardian era' – but his public and certainly more ostentatious
monarchy was in line with what the British public required.

Before considering Edward's role and his attitude to the
events of his time, one must remember that he was in a way a
very isolated figure, and that he came to the throne in late
middle age as a man who had long since developed his own
tastes and opinions. His closest confidants were often those who
had been with him as Prince of Wales – there was to be no
throwing over of previous companions as when Shakespeare's
Prince Hal became the upright Henry V. The new household
was made up from the officers of the Prince of Wales, and some
of Victoria's staff, such as Sir Arthur Bigge and William
Carington, were quietly demoted. Francis Knollys became
private secretary to the King, being given (to his chagrin,
since he wished to keep most of the duties of the secretary in
his own hands) Arthur Davidson and Frederick Ponsonby as
assistant private secretaries, in six-monthly alternation. Sir
Dighton Probyn became Keeper of the Privy Purse, although
in fact the King's financial affairs were also watched over by
Knollys, Lord Esher and Sir Ernest Cassel. Lord Esher was a
newer acquaintance, who had met the Prince for the first time
during his work for the Office of Works, but he made an
immediate impression and was appointed in 1901 Lieutenant
Governor of Windsor Castle.

These officers were in continual contact with the King. The
secretary's office dealt with all the important political correspondence, with ministers and the like. In 1906 Knollys
recalled: 'Lord Salisbury used to say, when Sir Henry Ponsonby
or Sir Arthur Bigge came to see him … "I wonder how much
of this is from the Queen and how much from Ponsonby and
Bigge?"' He himself was sometimes called 'the most powerful

Pieces of commemorative
china made for the 1902
coronation. The
coronation had to be
postponed once because
of the King's illness, to
the disappointment and
loss of the makers of the
china.

man in England'. The secretaries saw it as their duty to monitor the King's replies and where necessary to tone them down. During the tour of Italy in 1903, Ponsonby rephrased a reply to the minister who had advised the King against visiting the Pope. Had he not done so, he claimed, the minister would have had no alternative but to resign, such was the King's language. Ponsonby had learned from an earlier experience, when he had replied to a letter from Lord Roberts, concerning Sandhurst, in the *ipsissima verba* of Edward – only to be rebuked by the Commander-in-Chief that such a letter should be written by a private secretary. The duties of a private secretary are legion: but above all, discretion is the greatest virtue. They could thus defend Edward against the consequences of some of his spontaneous responses; although it is arguable that Knollys exceeded his brief in keeping information from the King during the crisis of the 1909 Budget, on the grounds that to have supplied it would have infuriated him even more with his ministers' behaviour.

The private secretary also kept an eye on events and brought to the attention of the King the questions that required a statement of his position. Thus, in 1904 Knollys telegraphed to the King, who was in Copenhagen, to inform him that, in asking Parliament to vote on the terms of the Anglo-French *entente*, Balfour, the Prime Minister, was entrenching on the power of the Crown to acquire and give up British territory. Edward replied, requiring an immediate confrontation with Balfour and an explanation.

Lord Esher, who worked on the Royal Commission of Inquiry into the South African War, became a permanent member of the Committee of Imperial Defence and was particularly influential. He had many contacts amongst politicians and reported regularly to Knollys and the King. To his natural love of backstairs intrigue (he refused a position in the Cabinet, preferring to play a more subtle role in events) Esher added a deep devotion to Edward and to the maintenance of the monarchic ideal, which he conceived of through the experience of Victoria's relationship with her ministers during the mid-nineteenth century. He edited the late Queen's letters in such a way as to emphasise the positive role she had played in policy-making at that time. Of course the King was never a tool either of Esher or of Knollys, and there were times when he severely disagreed with them, but they were the paramount influences on him during his reign and Cabinet ministers were aware that they had to deal not only with the monarch, but with two shrewd political realists, who saw to it that there was a royal opinion on every important issue and that that opinion was made known.

The work of the secretary was important because Edward had had little experience of constitutional procedure during his period as Prince of Wales. He preferred personal informal contact with ministers to regular audiences, whereas Knollys was trained in the language and protocol of correspondence with the Cabinet and prime ministers. According to Ponsonby, although Edward 'prided himself on being a constitutional monarch ... at heart he was an autocrat', and the presence of Esher and Knollys gave him a useful outlet for his frustration when ministers failed to modify their decisions according to his advice. In taking care of much of the King's correspondence and looking after his interests, Knollys performed great service. On a few occasions, however, the King's position was adversely affected. Knollys sometimes offered bad advice – such as his alarmist suggestion that the King should abdicate rather than submit to extortionate demands by the Government during the political crisis of 1909–10. Occasionally, too, the character and activities of the King's advisers were questionable; Esher's influence was much disliked and Knollys and Lord Farquhar, Master of the Household, were implicated in some rather shady financial dealings in Siberian mining shares.

The question of whether the King had an absolute right to participate in the making of Cabinet decisions, as opposed to being consulted afterwards, was not raised acutely during the reign, nor did Edward seek to do so. He knew a great deal of what went on before the official communications were written. Esher had his political contacts; Knollys was always well informed about Government thinking and Edward himself was often friendly with key figures, such as Sir John Fisher during the disputes of the Admiralty. On the other hand, although in the opening months of his reign Edward was delighted to be in receipt of so much information – he greatly impressed Lord Redesdale when he told him that he regularly devoted a few hours each night to reading despatches and papers – the early enthusiasm soon declined and the natural appetite for social pleasures and dislike of desk work confined him to covering issues of special interest, notably foreign and military matters. The early resolve, personally to sign the backlog of over six thousand army commissions which had built up at the end of Victoria's reign, yielded eventually to the use of a rubber stamp.

The experience of the first few months after his accession was clearly important in revealing to Edward the scope and limitations of his position. His accession was the first of a British sovereign not to force a dissolution of Parliament, and in the early months Edward kept a close eye on politics. Some of his suggestions to the elderly Lord Salisbury revealed a tendency towards excessive involvement; thus he proposed in March 1901 to ask Lord Rosebery to take over the leadership of the Opposition and in July he offered to send for Campbell-Bannerman to rebuke him after his 'methods of barbarism' speech on the Government's conduct of the South African War. Discreet hints from the Prime Minister that such interventions would be highly inopportune were enough to convince the King not to follow his inclinations. There were other difficulties with the form of the coronation oath, which still included a rabid anti-Catholic statement from the incoming monarch. During the ceremony in Parliament Edward read the part of the oath dealing with the repudiation of the Mass and the doctrine of transubstantiation in a noticeably low voice, and he found the behaviour of arch-Protestants like the Lord Chancellor, Lord Halsbury, most offensive. The cry of 'No popery!' was still potent, however, and the Government was unable to alter the form of the oath until after the accession of George v in 1910.

Although he had been dissuaded from rebuking Campbell-Bannerman, the King insisted on involving himself in the carrying on of the Boer War, which was in its last stages at the end of 1901. His suggestions could be valuable – Broderick, the Minister for War, praised his work in reforming the army medical system – but the Cabinet as a whole found Edward's support of a 'free hand' for Lord Kitchener, and his resentment that the terms of peace were discussed secretly in the Cabinet in 1902, at times an embarrassment. Conflict arose between them

'At heart he was an autocrat'

The Coronation

The ceremony was originally arranged for 26 June, but it had to be delayed because of the King's illness. Instead it took place on 9 August, but many of the foreign heads of State had already departed. Nevertheless the first coronation for over sixty years was made much of by the people of London.

ABOVE The invitation sent out by the Earl Marshal for the original date of the coronation, 26 June 1902.
RIGHT Biscuit box bearing the heads of Edward and Alexandra.

ABOVE Preparations made for the coronation in Piccadilly.

RIGHT The coronation procession passing through Parliament Square on its way to Westminster Abbey.

when the Government decided to appoint a Commission of Inquiry into the War, after the Boer surrender on 31 May 1902; Edward urged Salisbury not to 'do the army and also the country harm in the eyes of the civilised world'. As always, he regarded the washing of dirty linen in public as an unnecessary and self-humiliating operation. The demands of democratic politics, however, were on this occasion more important than the King's, and Salisbury went ahead with the inquiry. In a significant letter to Knollys, Edward wrote that the Cabinet 'is, apparently, so powerful a body that neither I nor the Prime Minister can gainsay them'.

No substantial disagreements occurred over the question of the King's finances. A Select Committee of the House of Commons was set up and Knollys had pleasure in reporting to it that 'for the first time in English history, the heir apparent comes forward to claim his right to the throne unencumbered by a single penny of debt'. This was only just accurate: Edward had no assets except the revenues from the duchy of Lancaster, since his mother's fortune had mostly gone to the younger children; but in any case, the passage of the finance proposals was smoother than expected. The Chancellor of the Exchequer offered to raise the royal income from the £385,000, which included £60,000 for the Privy Purse that had been granted to Victoria, to £470,000, together with an increase in the annuity to Queen Alexandra. Opposition from radicals like Labouchère and Keir Hardie proved ineffective. In the aftermath of the South African War such sums no longer seemed formidable and the bulk of the votes against the proposal came from the Irish members. Together with the raising of the income of the Prince of Wales to £90,000 a year, the arrangements proved satisfactory, although in 1907 there was an attempt by the Treasury to challenge the principle that the Government should pay for the expenses of royal visits to England. The idea that only visits of 'political importance' should be covered was firmly resisted by Knollys, who pointed out that 'His Majesty has his own views respecting the importance, from a political point of view, of visits of Foreign Sovereigns ... the Secretary of State might consider that they were not'. Since such a division of opinion might lead to conflict and since a bargain had been struck in 1901, the Treasury gave way.

Edward's first year as King was one of intense activity in many spheres. As well as his domestic efforts, there were the arrangements for the tour of the Duke of York in Canada and Australia. (Edward at first resisted the idea of his son going on such a long tour – but eventually agreed, since it had been one of Victoria's last wishes, and since the Government foresaw positive advantages in fostering imperial ties.) Then there were the King's two visits to Germany to attend the ailing Empress, his sister Victoria, and a minor crisis, when he handed the Kaiser a memorandum on Anglo-German relations prepared for him by Lord Lansdowne, instead of using it as a brief, as the Foreign Secretary had intended. (An indication of how closely he felt himself involved in day-to-day administration can be seen in the fact that Edward was very reluctant, while absent abroad, to appoint a member of the royal family to act in case of an emergency meeting of the Privy Council. He claimed he would always be ready to return should this become essential. By 1903, however, he was prepared to delegate the power to the Prince of Wales, and in 1906 he transferred the royal authority to the Prime Minister, the Lord Chancellor and the Lord President of the Council on the occasions when he and the Prince were both absent.) There was also in 1901 the regular visit to Marienbad in the company, among others of 'Mr A. Wagg, a racing man', and a stay at the *art nouveau* house of the Grand Duke of Hesse.

'His Majesty has his own views respecting the importance ... of visits of Foreign Sovereigns'

The stress of so much activity on top of his ordinary social routine produced signs of strain, and appendicitis developed in June 1902. The coronation had been arranged for 26 June and the King stubbornly insisted on its taking place on that date; but on 23 June he was told that if an operation was not performed, the peritonitis from which he was suffering would prove mortal. What was regarded then as very grave surgery lasted forty minutes and proved entirely successful; but the coronation arrangements had to be cancelled, to the chagrin of the delegations which had already arrived (and, incidentally, to the loss of the makers of commemorative china). It was enacted instead on 9 August in Westminster Abbey, and, although the King himself had to raise the frail eighty-year-old Archbishop of Canterbury from his knees at one point during the service, it passed off well, despite the absence of many of the

foreign princes who had returned home. The original contingent had included representatives from Russia, Korea, Zanzibar, as well as a host of European royalty, but they were scarcely missed by the public, eager to celebrate the end of the South African War at the recent conclusion of the Peace of Vereeniging, and the successful recovery of the King. As part of the celebrations a £30,000 banquet was given to the London poor and Queen Alexandra entertained 'the humble class of general servants in the metropolis'.

But what did this enthusiasm signify? Was Edward to have the power and dignity his mother had inherited when she swore her coronation oath in 1837, or was his influence to be limited to the essential but minor questions of the day? Was he to be a splendid figurehead, the symbol of the political stability of Britain and its Empire, rather than the man of affairs who would be hailed, as Albert had been, 'almost an informal member of the Cabinet'? By 1902, the minor questions already predominated. The King had been consulted about Church patronage and over the appointment of the successor to Lord Acton as Regius Professor of History at Cambridge. He took pleasure in teasing Salisbury about the 'trash' written by the Poet Laureate, Alfred Austin, although he agreed to let him retain his position on the change of sovereign – 'as long as he gets no pay ... the appointment was made by the Prime Minister'. On the other hand, Salisbury, with whom the King had great ties of mutual respect, was on the way out. Shortly before the coronation he resigned on grounds of health, leaving his place to his nephew, Arthur Balfour, whose interests were almost antithetical to those of the King, and who had less experience of dealing with the monarchy. It might be expected that the powers of the Crown, far from being advanced, would be yet further restricted. And this would probably have been true during the frequently factious years ahead, even if the King's real pleasure had not lain in fields outside the mainstream of party politics.

OPPOSITE Coronation portrait of Alexandra and Edward.

Ministers 1901-10

KING EDWARD'S REIGN spanned a crucial decade in the development of British government and politics, which witnessed the Conservative party split over Tariff Reform, the landslide victory of the Liberals in 1905 and their far-reaching programme of social reform, and the start of the bitter conflict between the House of Lords and the House of Commons, which led to the Parliament Act of 1911. Edward was the first monarch to come to the throne after the national political parties had developed, and after the widening of the franchise to include the greater part of the adult male population. Consequently, the story of his reign in home affairs is that of the attempt to reconcile the traditional power of his position with the necessities of administrations which were only symbolically 'the King's Government'.

The Crown had been removed from the political arena and the republican cry was long since dead, but the constitutional position of the King was by no means clear. Some contemporary commentators envisaged a wide role: in 1907 John Ward told The Trades Union Congress that Edward was 'almost our only statesman ... the greatest of our Kings since William the Conqueror', and Horatio Bottomley, maverick editor of *John Bull*, went so far as to assert that his abilities made Parliament 'almost a redundancy'. Cooler assessments revealed the limits. There could no longer be any question of a royal veto on Government legislation, nor, in practice, however stoutly he defended his right privately to comment on the actions of the Government of the day, could the King force the resignation of a minister or deflect the Cabinet from legislation it was determined to pursue. There was talk of abdication if Asquith's demands during the Parliament crisis of 1909–10 proved unreasonable, but it came from the household rather than from Edward himself. Such influence as the King did possess depended upon the potential 'nuisance' value of constant complaints about conduct of policy to the Prime Minister. No senior Cabinet minister owed his position solely to the support of the King, and in Cabinet consideration of important issues took place without regard to his opinion, the assumption being that once the decision had been taken, his consent would automatically follow. Thus, although Edward's staff often spoke of a deterioration in the position of the monarchy, there was no

PREVIOUS PAGES
'Edwardian Parade' by
Max Beerbohm. From
left to right: Edward VII,
unidentified, Joseph
Chamberlain, Henry
James, Lord Rosebery,
Reggie Turner, Arthur
Pinero, William
Rothenstein, George
Moore, Rudyard Kipling,
Lord Burnham, Winston
Churchill.

real effort to extend its powers, merely a concern that he should be treated with respect and that constitutional forms should be seen to be maintained – a primarily defensive position. (Searching for an example of the extension of the power of the monarch, Sir Sidney Lee could find only Edward's take-over of the duties of the Duke of Cambridge, when the latter died in 1904, as Ranger of the Royal Parks – scarcely a constitutional revolution!) Within these limits, however, Edward frequently made his views plain to the Government and the force with which he did so went far beyond what would be considered normal practice today. While his general concern related more to the constitutional forms than to the merits of issues, on military and naval matters his advice went much further and in this region of national security it is fair to speak of his positive influence on policy.

Whether or not Edward played any part in Salisbury's sudden decision to retire in 1902 (there were rumours of disagreement between them over foreign policy), he was precluded by his appendicitis from taking any active part in the Cabinet appointment of Arthur Balfour. The King was never happy with the new Prime Minister: Balfour was too much of a House of Commons man and, being both a dedicated politician and a political cynic, he was not inclined to pay undue attention to royal opinion. The King reciprocated the feeling. In 1903, when Balfour insisted on ratifying the Anglo-French *entente* by a vote in the House of Commons, the King, displeased at the affront to the royal prerogative, told Knollys: 'Mr Balfour has treated me with slight courtesy ... He is always so vague that probably he is wrong, but I must insist, and as a matter of principle, that he *admits* it.'

Bickering rather than quarrelling would be the best way to describe the relations between King and Prime Minister from 1902 until the Liberal victory at the end of 1905. The most outspoken dispute occurred with the Foreign Secretary, Lord Lansdowne, who had encouraged the Shah of Persia to make a state visit in 1902 in the expectation of being awarded the Order of the Garter, but without telling the King, in whose gift the Order was. Edward objected, not so much because the Shah was an infidel – Queen Victoria had given the Order to his father – as because the Foreign Office had failed to consult him.

Obstinately he refused to listen to Lansdowne's arguments and in the end the Shah had to leave, furious, and without the promise being fulfilled. Lansdowne was ready to resign, but his colleagues supported him. Knollys advised the King to give way: 'If he resigned, could the matter stop there in these days of Government solidarity?' In due course, the King relented and presented the Garter, but an ugly tone had made itself felt. In 1906 the Garter was given without fuss to the Emperor of Japan. A year later, however, the King of Siam visited England and in this case the Foreign Office agreed with the King in refusing. Harding minuted: 'Most people, I think, agree that it was a great mistake to have given the Garter of the late Shah of Persia.'

A more serious difference of opinion took place during the Tariff Reform crisis in 1903, after Joseph Chamberlain had opened out his scheme. The Conservative Cabinet was split and the King suggested that the issue should be referred to a Royal Commission. Balfour refused. The King's actions were inspired by awareness of constitutional problems rather than political considerations, although he himself inclined towards free trade, believing that the tariff programme was unsound in theory and politically inept. At the time of the mass resignations from the Cabinet in September 1903, the King felt that Balfour should have waited before giving the list of departing ministers to the press, as 'it would not look well in the eyes of the world that a matter of such importance should be settled without my having seen the Prime Minister'. There was further conflict over the appointment of ministers to replace those who had resigned, because the manner seemed to nibble at a right which the Crown had previously exercised.

Constant slight erosion of the Crown's prerogative irritated the King. He found it most distasteful when Balfour's arguments, after the Government's defeat in 1905 on the Irish Land Purchase Bill, seemed to imply that it lay wholly with the House of Commons to decide when a dissolution should take place. Later, as the Government staggered into its final crisis, the King urged Balfour either to meet Parliament or to dissolve – perfectly sound advice – and was piqued when the Cabinet decided instead to resign, hoping thereby to force the Liberals into taking office in a state of disunity. Balfour's

manoeuvre failed, but Edward had to accept, reluctantly; as Salisbury had pointed out in 1902, the Prime Minister could not 'interpose a (royal) veto against a decision taken by the Cabinet'. Edward himself realised that 'as a constitutional sovereign it is naturally not for the King to give advice to his Prime Minister in regard to the position of the Government'.

On the details of home affairs, the King showed himself far less concerned. The sectarian disputes over the Education Bill evidently bored him. He did, however, take an interest in South Africa and commended the policy of bringing Chinese labourers into the Transvaal, an issue against which the Liberals were to campaign with great success among British trades

The unfortunate visit of the Shah of Persia, which took place in 1902. The Shah expected to receive the Order of the Garter, but Edward resolutely refused to grant it to him. The royal party are seen on the King's yacht.

unionists. Edward declared himself 'delighted' when the policy was agreed and later noted his regret 'that so much heated opposition should have been shown to such a necessary measure'. But, as usual, on colonial matters as much as on home affairs, the proprieties concerned him more. He became angry that the Colonial Office should have offered a funeral with military honours after President Kruger's death without consulting him, and sent a magisterial rebuke to the Colonial Secretary, Lyttleton: 'He has acted quite out of order and not according to long established precedent. Queen Victoria would have strongly, and very strongly, resented such a proceeding.'

Questions of national security apart, the King's most useful function during the Balfour administration was probably in the carrying out of its Irish policy. Outraged at the behaviour of the Irish Nationalist MPs in cheering the news of a Boer victory in the later stages of the South African War, he had cancelled a projected tour of Ireland in 1902, but with the approval of George Wyndham, the new Irish Secretary, arrangements were made for a visit a year later. Happily this coincided with the passage of the Irish Education and Land Bills through Parliament, and, despite the perennial antagonism to royalty of the Dublin City Council, the King's reception was very favourable. Such enthusiasm had never been seen before in Dublin 'even for the late Queen'. With great tact Edward sent a message of condolence to the College of Cardinals on the recent death of the Pope – a gesture that was much appreciated among the Irish clergy and people. Throughout the tour there was a noticeable absence of ill-feeling, even during the visit to that notoriously anti-British city, Cork. The King's reception pleased the Government very much and Wyndham spoke of 'the dramatic and sympathetic completeness of the triumph which the King and Queen have won in Irish hearts'. Balfour, for once, offered his 'warmest congratulations'.

The King's interest in Irish affairs rose at once: he personally intervened in appointments at the Irish Office and he insisted on inserting a paragraph with a description of the Irish tour in the next King's Speech. In 1904, however, a crisis developed in the Unionist Party over the involvement of Sir Alexander MacDonald, Wyndham's Catholic Under-Secretary, in the

The old and new leaders of the Tory party – Lord Salisbury (above) who retired as Prime Minister in 1902, and Arthur Balfour (right) who succeeded him.

newly formed Irish Reform Association, which led eventually to Wyndham's resignation. Although he was perhaps the best Irish Secretary of his generation, the King was powerless to prevent this.

In general the King was antagonistic towards Balfour's manner and methods as Prime Minister. When it came to his attention that J. S. Sanders (Balfour's private secretary) had leaked some details about the King's Speech to the press, he commented acidly that: 'One has heard of the "New Woman" but he is the "New Man".' In 1905 Knollys wrote to Esher commenting that 'the difficulty the King has to contend with is that some Ministers settle questions ... without the King or anyone else knowing of it'. True, there was a steady stream of apologies from various ministers, but these often came *post facto*; and the ministers never had their political careers blighted because they had offended the royal sense of propriety.

Although relations between the King and his Prime Minister remained cold and unproductive, the King took up with enthusiasm the cause of military and naval reform. Edward had always been attracted towards questions of national security, even though he had been deprived of a military education; and with his experience of the status of the army in most European countries, to say nothing of his preference for the company of army officers, who formed much of his household, it is not surprising that Edward should have been gravely concerned at the deficiencies revealed during the South African War, and by the report of the subsequent inquiry. From the outset he was determined to be kept in full touch with Government thinking on the need for and shape of the resulting army reforms, and he informed Broderick (Minister of War since 1900): 'I shall ... always give you my heartiest support in all matters concerned with the army ... but at the same time you must expect criticism.'

Broderick, unfortunately, crossed swords with Lord Esher, now the King's unofficial adviser, and showed himself too slow in undertaking the reforms the King thought necessary. By 1903 his position had been seriously undermined by his failure to act on the recommendations of the Commission of Inquiry. Balfour and Lord Roberts also felt that Broderick was proving unsatisfactory and he was transferred to the India Office in the

Edward with his two surviving brothers in their military splendour. The Duke of Connaught, who became the Inspector General of the army in 1904, is in the middle and the Duke of Edinburgh on the right.

Cabinet changes of September 1903. Esher refused to accept the Secretaryship himself (preferring to wield a background influence) but the new appointment, H. O. Arnold-Foster, quickly proved responsive to the demand for reform. When the King suggested the appointment of a Committee to propose changes in the War Office, he agreed to place Esher and Sir John Fisher as the King's nominees on it. Edward himself played a role by persuading Balfour to act as chairman and he was well supplied with information on its proceedings. Early in 1904 the report was ready. Among its recommendations were the enlargement of the Committee of Imperial Defence and the establishment of an Army Council as the main source of authority in the future. The otiose post of Commander-in-Chief was to be scrapped. In the absence of any individual general of outstanding ability, there could be little objection to such a reform of the army structure and the King was further delighted when, as a result of his interventions, Lord Roberts decided not to become Inspector General, leaving the way clear for the appointment of his brother, the Duke of Connaught, to this prestigious, but largely honorary, position. Crown and Government were in complete agreement over the proposals and Balfour accepted the King's suggestion that the title of the War Office should be retained.

When the new Army Council turned to consider the detailed reforms, however, difficulties arose. The King began to complain to Arnold-Foster that he was not consulted and he cited precedents from his mother's reign. When the Council produced its scheme for reform of the whole service in July 1904, he gave the voluminous report his close consideration but he evidently still resented the fact that he had had little chance to comment while it was being drafted. As Knollys wrote to Arnold-Foster, this 'would have obviated the necessity of refusing his assent to certain proposals submitted in what is practically a final form' for, despite approval of the principle of decentralisation, the King found fault with certain proposals which involved the Treasury in the administration and discipline of the army. He also objected to the merging of the Aldershot and Salisbury Commands and wanted to lower the age for admission of subalterns to the Guards to eighteen years.

On the whole the Council resisted the King's criticisms but these were renewed when Arnold-Foster introduced his major scheme of army reorganisation in the Commons in July 1905. Although the reforms – the ending of the Cardwell system of linked battalions, and the provision for a regular army enlisted for nine years' service, with a home army serving two years with the colours, and six years in the reserve – were far-reaching, the King wanted something much more drastic. Knollys informed Balfour that 'the King cannot withhold his consent from the proposals which he is advised by the Cabinet to approve, but he cannot conceal his strong misgiving as to the effect which the announcement will have on the army, whom they will not reassure, and upon the public whom they will fail to satisfy'. Edward's opinion of Arnold-Foster fell yet further when he produced his pay scheme for army officers and presented some sections of the warrant as if the King had already consented to its provisions. Furious at the breach of etiquette, the King was not mollified by an apology and, in August 1905, he lent his support to moves to oust Arnold-Foster – although these fell through when Esher once again refused the offer of a Cabinet place.

A better relationship grew up between the King and R. B. Haldane, who became Secretary for War in the Liberal Government. Although disappointed because he had not been made Lord Chancellor, Haldane, who had been an active Liberal Imperialist, determined to carry through a more extensive plan of reform that would provide Britain with an efficient striking force and a competent reserve, and yet would, at the same time, satisfy his radical colleagues by reducing the army estimates. In this he established himself as one of the greatest reformers of the army. In the three years after 1906, the estimates were reduced by £2 million, but the Expeditionary Force was enlarged to 160,000 regulars. By the creation of a Territorial Reserve of fourteen organised divisions, the British army was turned into a substantial and efficient military unit. True it was still small by Continental standards, but it was splendidly equipped. When in 1908, with the King's full approval, the Committee of Imperial Defence decided that, in the event of war with Germany, the army should support the left flank of the French, it became possible to envisage Britain taking part in a European conflict as she had done in the latter part of the Napoleonic Wars. In all this, Haldane acknowledged that 'there was no minister who had greater cause to be grateful to his sovereign than himself'.

The King personally helped to support the Territorial and Reserve Forces Act by calling the Lords Lieutenant of the Counties to a meeting at Buckingham Palace, there urging on them the need to co-operate in forming the new County Associations. Overjoyed, Haldane wrote to assure him that 'a great impulse ... has been given to the movement for the organisation of a Territorial Army by the example which your Majesty has shown'. There was only one brief period of bad relations with Haldane, when the King came under the influence of Lord Roberts, who condemned as inadequate the training methods for the Territorials. Late in 1906 Edward began, in private, to refer to Haldane as 'a damned Radical lawyer and a German professor', and it seemed for a time that he would switch his influence to the support of Haldane's enemies, such as General Kitchener, who favoured an army raised by national conscription. At this point, Esher, now permanent secretary of the CID, intervened. Haldane was fighting a battle in the Cabinet simply to preserve the strength of the expeditionary force and the Territorials, and Esher hinted that he ought not to be attacked since 'so far no one has worked out a better plan ...'. He added, 'Haldane has done more for the Regular Army than any minister since Cardwell'. Although the King still feared that in default of an even larger army Britain was

'The King cannot withhold his consent'

'the laughing stock of the Continent', he saw the difficulties and let Haldane know privately that he had his full support during the Cabinet crisis over the estimates in June 1908.

Courtesy, as much as recognition, can be seen in some of the tributes paid to the King and a good deal was due to Esher's quiet insistence. Indeed, on certain matters, the King shows a curiously perverse streak, notably in his resistance to the change from scarlet uniforms to khaki. But in spite of the clash with Haldane over the proposed public inquiry into 'ragging' among the Scots Guards in 1907, where the King, once again, objected to 'washing dirty linen in public', he was prepared to throw his full social and personal influence behind schemes of reform and, in his concern to have an army capable of 'meeting a force of European picked troops', showed a grasp of the strategic realities across the Channel superior to that of many of the radicals in the Cabinet. By encouraging the early reform of the structure, the King played some part in creating not only the outstanding British Expeditionary Force but the stable conditions in which the army expanded after 1914.

Edward's devotion to the cause of army reform was matched by a close involvement in the affairs of the navy. Once again the Liberal Government sought to reduce the estimates and yet at the same time to increase efficiency, and once again the King's influence depended largely on his personal contacts, in this case with the key figure of Admiral Sir John Fisher. Fisher, who had done marvellous work in raising the morale of the Mediterranean fleet, was the coming man in the navy. In 1901 he became Second Sea Lord, Commander-in-Chief at Portsmouth in 1903, and First Sea Lord in 1904. He also became naval *aide-de-camp* to the King and worked closely with Esher (with whom he served on the Committee on War Office Reorganisation). Edward appreciated the extrovert character and good companionship of the tempestuous 'Jackie' Fisher – on one occasion Fisher suggested rolling the carpets back at Buckingham Palace for an impromptu dance and Edward agreed. At a rather dull dinner party Fisher livened up the occasion by singing off-key: 'We lives in Trafalgar Square, four lions they guard us there.' As early as 1904 Esher told the Admiral: 'The King will always back you.'

The stimulus of Fisher's policy came from the expansion of

'The King will always back you'

134

the German navy under the naval laws of 1898 and 1900, which appeared to threaten Britain's long nineteenth-century supremacy at sea. Under Lord Selborne, First Lord of the Admiralty, Fisher began the series of reforms which included the planning of the Dreadnought class, the most heavily-armoured battleship ever laid down. At the same time he pursued a policy of scrapping obsolete vessels and concentrated resources in home waters in order to confront the German High Seas Fleet. Fisher was convinced of the importance of winning the King's support for his plans and kept him fully informed of his ideas. So forceful a figure was he, that he threatened resignation if Walter Long – of whom he disapproved – was appointed First Lord after Selborne had retired, and won his case. He also succeeded in getting the King to appoint him as an additional Admiral of the Fleet so that he could stay on active service until 1911, instead of having to retire at the age of sixty-five in 1906. Some of Fisher's wilder ideas – notably his suggestion that the German fleet should be 'copenhagened' (that is, destroyed at its moorings by a sudden surprise attack) horrified the King, but on the whole Edward followed him, thinking that the menace of the German fleet ought to be countered. 'Our only probable enemy', Fisher wrote to the Prince of Wales, who had expressed certain objections, 'is Germany. We must therefore keep a fleet twice as powerful concentrated within a few hours of Germany.'

'The pruning knife ain't pleasant for fossils'

Fisher's dynamism and his passion for economy at the expense of less efficient sections of the navy, brought him many enemies. He might state baldly, 'The pruning knife ain't pleasant for fossils and ineffectives but it has to be used, and the tree is more vigorous for the loss of excrescences', but there were others, including Foreign Office officials, who thought that the re-allocation of squadrons would weaken the Empire and the network of imperial defence. (The naval estimates were reduced by £6 million from 1904–7. Thereafter, under the requirements of the Dreadnought programme, they rose by a total of £10 million by 1910.) Fisher's schemes for a 'nucleus crew' reserve force (as opposed to a full crew on an idle ship) was often criticised as unworkable and, suffering as he did from a succession of weak men as First Lords, Cawdor in 1905 and Lord Tweedmouth from 1905 to 1908, Fisher needed the

Quarrels over naval policy developed during the middle of Edward's reign. On one side stood Admiral Sir John Fisher (right), with his ideas of economy and reliance on the Dreadnought. Opposing him was Edward's former friend, Admiral Charles Beresford (opposite), who posed as advocate of increased naval spending and widening of naval strength.

King's support against the antagonistic group which grew up after 1906 around the leadership of Admiral Lord Charles Beresford.

Beresford, then Commander-in-Chief in the Mediterranean, began a campaign of insubordination, in which he roused the support of the traditionalists in the Admiralty, 'the Blue Funk School' or 'the Yellow Admirals' as those in the 'Fishpond', Fisher's supporters, called them. A legacy of the old enmity between Edward and Lord Charles may be seen in the way the King squashed the campaign against Fisher, waged by Beresford's society followers, such as Lady Londonderry. But the opposition did not end there. Beresford, who had claims to the post of First Sea Lord himself, was as much a master of publicity and intrigue as Fisher and continued to protest even after his transfer to command of the Channel fleet. In the

restricted social circle from which the Admiralty command was drawn (it was not until McKenna became First Lord in 1908 that the Minister for the Navy sat in the House of Commons), the Crown could tip the balance in favour of Fisher and eventually the Fisherites got Beresford dismissed. But Beresford carried his vendetta into the political arena and appealed to Balfour and Asquith for a public inquiry into the Fisher strategy. He posed as an advocate of increased naval spending and deplored the policy of total reliance on the Dreadnought as likely to undermine Britain's lead in conventional naval forces. It was felt that Germany might attain parity in ordinary battleships by 1912 and the 'We want eight and we won't wait' groups like the Imperial Maritime League advocated both increased naval spending *and* the dismissal of Fisher. 'We arraign John Fisher', cried the *Daily Express*, 'at the bar of public opinion … with the imminent possibility of national disaster.' Under considerable pressure, Asquith agreed to the inquiry and also, much more weakly, conceded Beresford's objections against the appointment of Lord Esher to the sub-Committee of the CID which investigated the charges. The CID eventually reported that the criticisms were largely unjustified and that the fleet was overwhelmingly superior to any threat, but it criticised the Admiralty for their factions and for not taking Beresford into their confidence. Their recommendation in favour of a Naval General Staff, which Fisher had always resisted, and the crisis itself undermined Fisher's position. Although the King had told Knollys that 'Fisher shall not be kicked out in spite of the Cabinet, the press and Charles Beresford', Fisher was not backed strongly enough by the Government and in January 1910, six months after the report, he resigned.

Nevertheless, Fisher's policy remained intact and in time was vindicated by the success of the navy in protecting the coast of Britain from invasion during the 1914–18 War. The technical details, of course, owed little to the King's inspiration – Esher told Fisher not to be concerned that the King seemed unable to grasp details, 'his life is too full for that, but he will always say to himself, "Jack Fisher's view is so and so, and he is sure to be right"'! But his favour did much to keep Fisher in authority. Fisher himself never forgot. 'When your Majesty

'Revilers would have eaten me but for your Majesty'

138

backed up the First Sea Lord against unanimous feeling against the Dreadnought ... when your Majesty launched her, went to sea in her, witnessed her battle practice ... it just simply shut up the mouths of the revilers (who) would have eaten me but for your Majesty', he wrote in 1907, and later in his memoirs he opened with a description of Edward's 'unfaltering support ... though every sycophantic effort was exhausted in an endeavour to alienate him from support of me'.

By natural inclination, military and naval matters absorbed more of the King's attention than most of the other issues of political life. Yet the change of Government after the 1905 general election, with its overwhelming majority for the Liberals, provided a difficult exercise in the royal prerogative. The choice of a successor to Balfour seemed simple. Sir Henry Campbell-Bannerman had been Liberal leader since 1899 and, although he had offended the King by his choice of the phrase 'methods of barbarism' to describe the concentration camps used in the South African War, this appointment appeared politically inevitable. But within the Liberal party a powerful group, consisting of Asquith, Haldane and Sir Edward Grey – all of whom had roots in the Liberal Imperialist organisations – had made a private agreement (the Relugas Compact) to force Campbell-Bannerman to accept a peerage on becoming Prime Minister, thus leaving Asquith as Leader in the House of Commons. Haldane believed that 'to place this on a sure foundation ... we needed the sympathy and possible co-operation of King Edward'.

Edward ignored the manoeuvre. Esher gave him elaborate advice on the correct procedure to follow and the King was probably more influenced by the views of Dr Ott about Campbell-Bannerman's state of health than the activities of the group. Knollys actually encouraged Haldane to serve under Campbell-Bannerman on the grounds that to refuse would embarrass the King and leave the Prime Minister with too many radical colleagues. In the event, the Relugas Compact collapsed in the face of Campbell-Bannerman's determination to form a Government on his own terms and because Asquith was not prepared to press him unduly. During the formation of the Cabinet Edward interfered little and the new Prime Minister remarked that the King 'had been first rate through it all'.

On only one other occasion did the King have to use his power to appoint a Prime Minister. In 1907 it was obvious that Campbell-Bannerman's health was declining and Lord Esher noted that the King 'would exercise his prerogative unaided' in choosing his successor. The choice, however, was obvious, as soundings by Knollys soon revealed, Asquith being heir apparent. By February 1908 when Campbell-Bannerman was confined to bed in Downing Street, Asquith had already assumed the function of sending Cabinet reports to the King. The actual time of the change-over presented some problems, however, as the King was preparing to leave in March for a visit to Biarritz. Asquith promised that if necessary he would come out to France to receive the premiership from the King and the Cabinet changes would wait until they had returned. Soon afterwards, Campbell-Bannerman sent his letter of resignation to the King, and Knollys (who was in England) advised Edward to return to London in the interests of convenience and constitutional propriety. Pleading reasons of health, Edward insisted on Asquith's fulfilling his promise and Asquith came, despite the complaints of those who considered his absence inopportune during crucial debates on the Licensing Bill. For the first time since the days of Lord Chatham, an incoming Prime Minister kissed hands on foreign soil; and among a deal of criticism *The Times* called it 'an inconvenient and dangerous departure'. Little harm was done – but the incident perhaps throws light on where the priorities of the King lay.

In contrast with his relationship with the Conservative Government, Edward got on well at first with the Liberal party who were in office throughout the rest of his reign. His advisers, Knollys and Esher, were men of mild Liberal persuasion and Campbell-Bannerman himself was often more willing to respect the King's views than Balfour had been. Although there was slight friction over the exercise of the Prime Minister's patronage, and although the wishes of the King were sometimes overridden with regard to political appointments to his household, the King was friendly with the bluff, hearty Scotsman. In 1908 he told Knollys that 'it would be a bad day for the country if anything happened to Campbell-Bannerman';

OPPOSITE A cartoon from *Punch*, 1908. Asquith took over the leadership of the Liberal party and the premiership on the resignation of Campbell-Bannerman.

ASQUITH'S GREAT CABINET PUZZLE.

(With acknowledgments to the " Answers " Elephant.)

141

and when Sir Henry resigned he wrote to him, saying that 'it has always been a great pleasure and satisfaction for me to do business with you at all times'. With Asquith, relations were not so cordial. The King thought him secretive and reserved, and resented his constant assurances that he did not want to trouble the King with difficult matters, suspecting, correctly, that they meant that he was withholding information. When he told Esher that Asquith was 'deficient in manners, but in nothing else', Esher understood very well that manners could be of the essence of judgment. Campbell-Bannerman may have been naturally indolent about providing information about the Cabinet discussions to the King, but Asquith's policy was deliberately to doctor the reports in order to highlight what he thought would interest the King and to exclude more contentious subjects. Thus he gave prominence to the reward offered for the Crown jewels of Ireland (which had been stolen just before the King's visit there in 1907), rather than the contemporary discussion on the provision of old age pensions.

The King tolerated rather than admired Asquith but he came to regard with great antipathy the activities of the radicals, in particular Lloyd George, whose fiery condemnation of the House of Lords, opposition to increased military estimates (particularly during the Cabinet struggle over the number of Dreadnoughts to be built in 1908) and advocacy of Anglo-German *rapprochement*, made him something of a *bête noire*. During the passage over the 1906 Education Bill, Lloyd George had referred to the issue as being 'whether the country is to be governed by the King and his peers, or by the King and his people' and Campbell-Bannerman had to apologise – not for the last time – for the use of such language by a Cabinet minister. Lloyd George became Chancellor of the Exchequer in 1908, but in spite of occasional glimpses of warmth the King refused to entertain him as minister in attendance on any of the royal tours or functions. Antipathy towards him and his close colleague, Winston Churchill, the Home Secretary, tended to influence the King towards acceptance of Asquith as a check against radical policies likely, in his opinion, to damage the harmony of society and weaken national security. The rise of men like Lloyd George from lowly origins to high positions of authority spelt out the changing nature of political life and

Two members of the
Liberal Government who
preached a crusade against
property and poverty
with their Budget of 1909,
a campaign which the
King sought to restrain.
LEFT Winston Churchill
in 1904, when he was MP
for Oldham.
BELOW David Lloyd
George in 1910.

the steady erosion of the function of aristocracy within the Government; it was not a development with which Edward had much sympathy.

In the face of the great reforming legislative programme of the Liberals, the King showed himself increasingly conservative. He expressed hostility to the principle of legalised picketing (refusing to recognise that any picketing could be 'peaceful') in the 1906 Trades Disputes Act, and he opposed staunchly the movement in favour of women's suffrage. Campbell-Bannerman was taken heavily to task for some articles that he had written giving mild support. The behaviour of the suffragettes, Edward fulminated, 'has been so outrageous and does their cause (for which I have no sympathy) much harm'. He was horrified when Lloyd George appeared on the platform of a women's suffrage meeting at the Albert Hall – 'a most improper thing', he wrote to Asquith, 'as it showed an entire absence of good judgement, good taste and propriety. I shall have no more to do with him than is absolutely necessary'. For different, strategic reasons he also objected to a Channel tunnel, proposals for which were before the Government in 1907.

The most significant dispute, which clouded over the last two years of the reign, was the growing tension between the House of Lords and the Commons. In the aftermath of electoral defeat, Balfour had threatened that the Unionist party still 'would continue to control the destiny of this great Empire' and the House of Lords had begun thereafter to reject or seriously amend most of the Liberal measures that were sent up from the Commons. In order not to lose working-class support, the peers let through the Trades Disputes Act which undid the harm done to unions by the Taff Vale judgement, but they destroyed a Plural Voting Bill and in 1906 threatened to throw out the Education Bill prepared by Augustine Birrell. There were certain constitutional precedents for such behaviour. The Lords were particularly keen in recalling their role in destroying the legislation, including the second Home Rule Bill, of the 1892–5 Liberal Government. In that case their activity had been partly justified by the Unionist victory at the polls at the next election. But in 1906 they were treating with contempt a massive Liberal majority elected only a year before.

Given his view of the role of the monarchy in maintaining

the balance of interest in society, it was not unreasonable that the King should feel that he must strive for a compromise between the Houses. The example of Victoria's interventions in the disputes over the Disestablishment of the Church of Ireland in 1869 and the Reform Bill crisis in 1884 were very much within his memory. Over the actual principle of the 1906 Education Bill, the King stood closer to the position of the Anglican bishops who were determined to wreck it. 'Most unfair', he commented, after seeing its terms. 'Instead of smoothing matters, it will produce violent dissension between the Church of England and the Roman Catholics on one side, and the nonconformists on the other.' To Esher he wrote, 'What can the Government be thinking of in excluding teaching religion in our schools? Do they wish to copy the French!' Nevertheless, Edward believed that deadlock between the Houses would be 'a most regrettable situation', and in November 1906 he secured the attendance of the Archbishop of Canterbury at all Cabinet discussions of the bill. Despite this, and a series of personal meetings between Campbell-Bannerman and the bishops, compromise proved impossible. Religious education was too politically contentious a subject in the constituencies, and the Conservatives had decided that any attempt to remodel the terms of their own 1902 Act should fail. The Lords made wrecking amendments and the Commons rejected them. The Tory Lord Lansdowne refused to negotiate with the Liberal Lord Crewe and the bill lapsed. Its death and the consequent rebuff to nonconformist opinion left a long legacy of bitterness between the Liberals and the House of Lords and before the session ended Campbell-Bannerman threatened that 'the resources of the constitution' were not exhausted.

'It showed an entire absence of good judgement, good taste and propriety'

The King approved of the hereditary principle but he believed more strongly in the virtues of conciliation. He feared the activities of the extremists on both sides but he was appalled chiefly by the unreasonableness of the Tory leaders (encouraged by Unionist successes in by-elections) in refusing to moderate their opposition to selected Liberal measures. In June 1907, Campbell-Bannerman's resolutions, declaring the Government's intention to introduce a bill to reduce the power of the Lords from that of rejection to one of delay, were carried in the Commons. In clear defiance, the Lords threw out the Small-

GUNPOWDER for the HOUSE of LORDS. Novem^r 1907 C.B

THE NEW GUY FAWKES PLOT;

OR, THE BEST ADVERTISED CONSPIRACY IN THE WORLD.

[The First Autumn Meeting of the Cabinet has been summoned for the Fifth of November, Guy Fawkes Day.]

Punch cartoon of October 1907 showing the Liberal Government preparing to blow apart the House of Lords with their new measures. The barrel is being drawn by Campbell-Bannerman to the left, and Lloyd George to the right.

holdings (Scotland) and Land Values (Scotland) Bills, and also repudiated Bills for Welsh Disestablishment and Licensing Reform. In 1908, the King's attempts at conciliation on a more moderate Education Bill failed again. No trouble was expected with the Lloyd George Budget in 1909, however. The taxation measures were stiff (income tax was raised to 1s 2d in the pound, surtax was introduced on incomes in excess of £5,000 a year, and new taxes were projected on the unearned increment from land) but the Lords had not rejected a Finance Bill for more than a century.

The Budget was intended to outbid the competing programme of social reform on which the Unionists had won a whole run of by-elections, and some of its provisions, such as land taxes, seemed to be directed straight at the recalcitrant peers, on whom in his polemics Lloyd George heaped ridicule.

146

Some peers, in return, claimed that the land tax constituted a 'social revolution' and thus entitled them to treat the Budget as an extraordinary event. The King's own rather illogical objections to the Budget ('What would happen to land if these taxes were pressed upon it in time of war?' he asked Asquith) were soon dwarfed by the prospect that the Upper Chamber might reject it on the grounds that such a radical measure demanded a general election. Through the summer of 1909, as the Bill ground slowly through the Commons, the danger increased and towards the end of the year Edward sought out experts on the constitutional position. While agreeing with the Liberal Reginald McKenna that rejection would be in breach of constitutional precedent and would create serious problems for the Government in raising revenue, the King also discussed the hypothesis with Lord Cawdor and the Unionist leaders Balfour and Lansdowne (scrupulously obtaining Asquith's permission to take a personal sounding). The Unionists stood firm, much to the King's distaste; they would reject the Budget and in late November the Lords did so by a huge majority. Asquith asked for, and was granted, the dissolution of Parliament.

The King's constitutional position was now as unclear as that of the Lords had been in rejecting the Budget. The experts argued: Sir F. Pollock held that the rejection was in breach of the constitution, Professor Dicey and Sir William Anson considered it quite legitimate. Meanwhile the issue at stake soon widened into a comprehensive discussion on the right of a Liberal majority in the Commons to see its legislation take effect. Lloyd George and Churchill boldly cast the debate as part of the war between property and poverty – although the new revenue in the Budget was intended as much to meet the cost of increased naval estimates as of the new old age pension scheme. The King made efforts to restrain such acrimony; Knollys wrote to Crewe in August 1909 to say that the King protested against ministers' speeches 'full of false statements, of socialism in its most insidious form'. The thrust was aimed at Lloyd George for his famous attack on the peers made at Limehouse. True, Edward also deplored the 'foolish and mean speeches and sayings' of 'great landowners and capitalists' such as Lord Willoughby de Broke and Lord Rothschild, but it was Lloyd George in particular whom he cautioned against

THE TACTICIAN.

THE BUDGET BOY. "BUT SUPPOSING HE WANTS TO EAT ME UP?
UNCLE ASQUITH. "IT'LL BE THE GREATEST MISTAKE HE EVER MADE IN HIS LIFE. I'VE ONLY BEEN WAITING FOR A READ
D EXCUSE TO DESTROY HIM."

Punch cartoon of September 1909, depicting the wily Asquith pushing his Budget towards the lion – the House of Lords.

inflaming 'the passions of working and lower orders against people who happen to be owners of property'. Knollys saw that the King was annoyed when he was assumed to be opposed to what the Lords had done. Their action certainly increased the likelihood of the King being dragged into the arena of party politics. Quite apart from his natural inclinations, the course of events presented him with a most difficult choice. In early December the Cabinet considered courses of action if the Lords rejected the Budget again, after a Liberal majority had been returned at the election. One solution envisaged was to remove from the Crown the right to create peers, or else to obtain a guarantee that the King would create enough Liberal

148

peers to carry the Budget through. When Knollys heard of these discussions (via Esher and Haldane) he decided not to inform the King 'as it would be a mistake to set him still more against his ministers'. It was at this time that whispers of abdication, should the Government demand too much, began to be heard.

The result of the January election was most unsatisfactory from Asquith's point of view, although as Esher saw, it weakened the Government's hand against the King, While the Liberals still held a majority over the Unionists, they depended upon the support of the Irish Nationalists for a stable Government. The Irish, while keen on reforming the House of Lords in order to allow a Home Rule Bill to pass, had certain objections to parts of the Budget. As a result, there was a danger that the Finance Bill might not get to the Lords at all. The uncertain balance also gave the lie to Asquith's claim that the Liberals had the means to press through a Bill to deal with the powers of the Lords – because on this issue, the King had quite specifically refused to give Asquith a guarantee to create peers, unless a second general election were held. Balfour waited in the wings, ready all the time to form a minority Government if Asquith were to request guarantees which the King decided to refuse. Edward was well aware of the situation and wrote in the aftermath of the election, 'The Government may not last'.

When Parliament met in February 1910, Asquith admitted that he had no pledge from the King to create peers to force through a Parliament Bill, and he added that to ask for one before the Bill itself had been prepared would be unreasonable. However, in order to persuade the Irish to support him in the Commons over the Budget, Asquith had to bring in a measure to curb the Lords as soon as possible. On 14 April he introduced the Parliament Bill, whose preamble stated that it was intended 'to substitute for the House of Lords a Second Chamber constituted on a popular basis'. The Lords were refused the right to reject money bills, and in future were to be permitted only a suspensory veto over other legislation, which would become law (the Royal Assent having been declared) after two years had elapsed between its introduction and the third reading in the Commons. The Bill also reduced the life of Parliaments from seven to five years.

The constitutional crisis seemed about to break. Convinced

that Asquith was determined, as he stated in the Commons on 14 April, to see that Government policy received 'statutory effect in this Parliament', the Irish came into line over the Budget. But whatever the Lords did with the Finance Bill, they would inevitably reject the Parliament Bill in the form in which it had been presented. The King was in a dilemma. He had failed to persuade Balfour to accept the verdict of the election and allow the Finance Bill through the Commons. Consequently the Irish had been committed to a quarrel which only marginally concerned them, but with the result of bolstering the Liberal strength. But while the King might deplore Unionist intransigence, he liked the Liberal solution even less. In January he told Lord Crewe that he was most unwilling to create life peers to fill the new Chamber; yet his own plan (which involved the limitation of voting in the Lords to one hundred peers chosen by the party leaders) had been passed over on the grounds that it would mean that the vote would be given to party hacks rather than men of principle. In February the King's Speech referred to the measures to reconstitute and redefine the powers of the Lords as 'necessary ... in the opinion of my advisers' – a phrase which seemed to indicate personal hesitancy. Edward had been absent in Biarritz through most of March and April, but it was clear that he must be ready to act if Asquith, as he had promised the Commons, should 'tender such advice to the Crown which will have to be taken if policy is to receive statutory effect'.

At least two choices existed: a referendum (increasingly unlikely in view of the Irish feelings) or a demand for the creation of peers; and either might take the form of 'advice' which a constitutional monarch would be bound to accept from his Government. But the Lords were certain to reject the Bill, just as Asquith was committed to action within the life of that Parliament. Given that the King had already declared that he would give no guarantees until a second general election had been held, this time on the Parliament Bill, there seemed to be no possible way out except by a war of constitutional attrition. To discuss a solution, Knollys, Esher, Balfour and the Archbishop of Canterbury met in a rather conspiratorial conclave at Lambeth Palace at the end of April, when it was apparent that the Lords would pass the Budget with the minimum of fuss.

Esher supported the unconventional idea that the King could reject the advice of his ministers, if it was unpalatable, and that he had a right to call on Balfour to form an administration – which Balfour was quite prepared to do. The last time that a Government with a majority in the Commons had thus been overthrown by the action of the Crown, however, was when William IV made the ill-fated decision to call on Peel in 1834, and, indeed, Balfour declared the 'future of the monarchy itself' might depend on how Edward replied when the demand was made.

Parliament went into recess after the Royal Assent had been given to the Budget. Knollys was still searching for a way to introduce a referendum as an acceptable solution of the conflict. Among all the possibilities, however, one had been ignored: that the decision would not have to be taken while King Edward was still alive. The King collapsed on the afternoon of 6 May and after a series of heart attacks, died later that night. All political calculations which depended on the personal commitments of the leaders and the King, as well as on party political considerations, were shattered.

THE POLITICAL CRISIS of 1909 was certainly not of the King's choosing and the circumstances were most distressing to him. Whatever his natural inclination might have been, he strove to play the part of constitutional sovereign; but he never pretended that he was as interested in this or any of the aspects of home policy of his governments, except military and naval matters, as he was in foreign affairs. He delighted in diplomacy, believing that he had a distinctive contribution to make in the development of British foreign policy – and in many ways this was true. It had been the only subject of continuing interest through the barren years as Prince of Wales and since the 1890s Edward's practical knowledge had been bolstered not only by his contacts abroad, particularly in France, but by access to Cabinet information.

In his approach to the conduct of diplomacy, the King had to acknowledge the peculiar nature of the making of foreign policy. Unlike policy, say, on education, where the minister responsible had to take into consideration the conflicting views of Anglicans, Roman Catholics and nonconformists, foreign policy, while theoretically representing the will of the whole nation, followed definitions of British interests and commitments laid down by a very narrow circle, composed of Foreign Office officials and the Foreign Secretary himself. The views of other departments, particularly the armed services, were taken into account but the Foreign Secretary had a wide sphere of autonomy in Cabinet and tended to rely on the Prime Minister to back him up in ensuring his colleagues' acquiescence. During the 1901–10 period, foreign policy was not regarded as an aspect of party politics and the virtues of continuity tended to override ideological feelings on most issues except that of the South African War.

Democratic checks on the conduct of foreign policy remained remote, even after the end of the 1914–18 War. Consequently power to make policy lay very largely with the Foreign Secretary and Foreign Office. In theory, the King had the right personally to conclude treaties, declare war, make peace and cede territory, but in fact these functions had steadily been taken over during the nineteenth century. More important, the Crown's influence in determining the definitions of British interests on which the structure of diplomatic activity was

PREVIOUS PAGES Edward was linked by kinship to most of the crowned heads of Europe and consequently was able to help considerably in carrying out British foreign policy. From left to right: Queen Ena of Spain, King Edward, Empress Frederick of Germany, Kaiser William II, Queen Alexandra, the Queen of Portugal, King Alfonso of Spain, Queen Maud of Norway.

154

erected, had also been eroded, partly, at least, by the sheer complexity of business at the turn of the century. These factors, however, did not exclude the role of the sovereign as an influence and as the instrument of action.

Edward consistently accepted the view of British interests propounded by his Foreign Secretaries and although there were points of disagreement when he felt that his position was being used, such as the award of honours to foreign heads of State, or when the prerogative was whittled down, as in the Asquith Government's decision to cede territory in Somaliland to France in 1909 by decision of the Cabinet, he never refused a request for assistance in carrying out the Government's chosen policy.

But the European scene offered a contrast. Before 1914 the principal European countries were, with the exception of France, monarchical, and their external policy lay very much in the hands of royalty. Although he exaggerated his own power, Kaiser William declared in 1901: 'I am the arbiter and master of German foreign policy and the country *must* follow me.' Certainly his ministers held office at his pleasure. In 1909 the Kaiser told Edward that he was going to get rid of Chancellor von Bülow, and the Chancellor was duly sacked. In the empires of Russia and Austria, the question of democratic checks did not arise at all, and ministers depended very largely on the favour of royalty. Edward drew no distinction between Isvolsky and the Czar, or Aerenthal and Franz Joseph.

By temperament Edward was inclined to see the practice of diplomacy in the terms which had characterised the Congress of Vienna in 1815. By birth, too, he was intimately involved in the links of royal relationships – the Kaiser was his nephew, the Czar his wife's nephew, Frederick VIII of Denmark and George I of Greece his brothers-in-law, the future Haakon VII of Norway his son-in-law, to say nothing of distant links with Leopold of Belgium, Carlos of Portugal, Ferdinand of Bulgaria and Alfonso of Spain. Consequently he was afforded a powerful place in the system that lubricated European affairs by his visits to and his entertaining of powerful royal relations. In that world policies and attitudes were moulded, not only in Cabinets between ministers in diplomatic notes and correspondence, but through the meetings of heads of State. It is easy to

'He never refused a request for assistance in carrying out the Government's chosen policy'

criticise the methods of pre-war European diplomacy – over all the dynastic manoeuvres of those years hangs the spectre of the 1914-18 War – but the system was all that European statesmen had to work with, and it was one in which Edward might expect to play an important role; if not the role of the autocrat, at least that of the representative of British government policy. How far he took a part and how important it was, can be seen through three different stages of the making of foreign policy: his own personal adherence to a continuous programme; the extent of his influence on ministers and Cabinet; and the significance given by foreign observers to what the King was actually doing, as an indication of British policy on which to base their own reactions.

In 1901, at the start of the reign, Europe was dominated by the Dual (Russia and France) and Triple (Germany, Austria and Italy) Alliances; but these were not yet the rigid systems that were to determine the pattern of conflict in 1914. More significant, at the turn of the century, was the feeling of Continental solidarity based on a common dislike of Britain. France and Russia had suffered diplomatic reverses with Britain over colonial disputes and both countries displayed a sympathy for the Boers which was greatly resented by the King and his ministers. Lord Salisbury's policy of 'splendid isolation' seemed responsible for the nadir reached in British diplomatic fortunes, and within the Government circle it was widely believed that Britain must make new friends on the Continent to revive her influence.

Although Germany had already begun the programme of naval building it seemed that the absence of other sources of hostility might warrant an overture for the Anglo-German Alliance which had been canvassed by British statesmen since 1899. Edward was at first enthusiastic about improving Anglo-German relations, influenced not least by his profound mistrust of Russian ambitions. In the aftermath of Victoria's death, the behaviour of the Kaiser seemed to give encouragement to prospects of ending Britain's isolation and Baron von Eckhardstein (Secretary at the German embassy) noted the 'full and sincere understanding' between the King and the Kaiser. On 27 January 1901, at a luncheon with the King, William

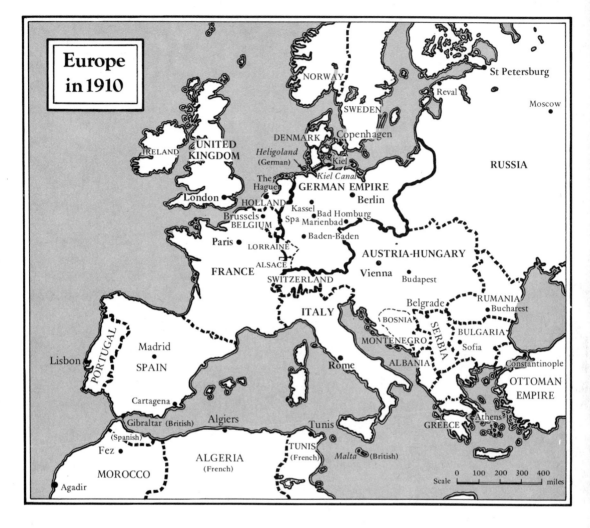

Europe in 1910

spoke of the benefits of an alliance of the 'two teutonic nations', holding out the prospect of European peace secured by the might of German arms and the British navy – although a long-term view might have raised doubt about the traditional balance of power policy when confronted with such a grouping.

Anglo-German approaches were doomed to failure, however, no matter how sincere the King's desire. Edward made two visits to Germany in 1901, where discussion of diplomacy was combined with family concern over the declining health and death of Victoria, the Emperor's mother and Edward's sister. Neither of these visits was easy: Edward committed the minor gaffe of handing over his Foreign Office brief and, worse, the tension that was always present when the two monarchs met showed itself only too clearly when William spent most of an important interview declaiming against the perfidy of the British Government and complaining that Edward was not fully informed of the terms of the Anglo-Japanese agreement, then under negotiation. Although the King was prepared to overlook the personal failings of his nephew, who favoured him, for example, with a letter which spoke of British ministers as 'unmitigated noodles', the tide was running against any permanent understanding. Late in 1901 Joseph Chamberlain, the Colonial Secretary, who had previously been a firm advocate of agreement, began to tire of German reticence. In a public speech he pointed out the hostility of the German press towards the British effort in South Africa and he refused to accept criticism from Germans, who, he said, were guilty of conduct just as bad 'in Poland, in the Caucasus, in Algeria, in Tongkin, in Bosnia, in the Franco-Prussian War'. Although Edward reaffirmed, through the British ambassador in Germany, his desire for 'a thorough *entente cordiale*' with the Kaiser, relations were now rapidly cooling and von Bülow firmly repudiated what Chamberlain had said.

The growing estrangement was not healed by the Kaiser's chilly reception at Sandringham in 1902, although the German ruler drew a distinction between the King, as the lesser of two evils, and Chamberlain, 'whom we wish to go to a hotter place'. In February 1902, Chamberlain had met the French ambassador, Cambon, at a Marlborough House dinner party and Eckhardstein had noticed them discussing the situation in Morocco and Egypt. It was the first overt sign of friendship with France. After the party, the King had called Eckhardstein in and warned him: 'We are being urged more strongly than ever by France to come to an agreement with her in all colonial disputes.' Already the negotiations for a defensive alliance with Japan had been successfully concluded. The Boer War was coming to an end. Thus Edward's phrase can be seen as a last appeal to Germany to come to terms. If friendship was rejected, he would have no choice but to take advantage of what could be obtained from having France as a partner instead. And this was not merely a matter of the King's friendship with French politicians; he was in the closest accord with the thinking of

158

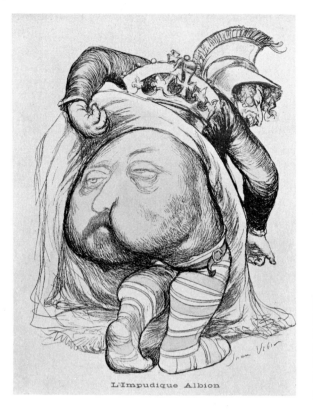

L'Impudique Albion, the
French attitude towards
Edward and England at
the beginning of his reign
is shown in this caricature
from L'Assiette au Beurre,
published in 1903.

Lansdowne and the Conservative Government. When the
Sultan of Morocco sent a delegation to the King bearing a
personal petition on the subject of a loan, he handled its reception with discretion and with the constant advice of Lansdowne.

Edward now began to prepare for what was to be his most
outstanding foray into the diplomatic sphere. Right in the
middle of the flux, as the British Government prepared to
change horses, he charted out the itinerary for his state tour of
1903 without the aid of any Cabinet advisers. The prospect was
rather daunting for the Foreign Office – Victoria had made only
one official visit abroad, to Paris in 1855. It had been obvious
that Edward's eagerness for foreign travel in Europe would
provide opportunities for contact with other heads of State, of
potential value to the development of British foreign policy.
But in this case the omens seemed unfavourable, and in order
to keep the visit in a minor key the Foreign Office saw fit to
provide as minister plenipotentiary to accompany the sovereign,
to converse with foreign diplomats and to report back to the

159

Foreign Office, merely an Assistant Under Secretary, the Hon. Charles Hardinge, whose wife was one of Queen Alexandra's ladies-in-waiting. Perhaps they expected nothing to happen. The first part of the tour, which included visits to Portugal and Italy (as well as to Gibraltar and Malta), presented few problems and confirmed the innocuous nature of the tour. At all points Hardinge's well-written speeches provided acceptable bromide. The reference to 'our respective countries and colonies, the integrity and preservation of which is one of my dearest aims and objects' did much to please Portuguese imperialist sentiment, and in Rome Edward made a timely reference to the shared ideals of liberty and civilisation held in Italy and Britain alike. But after a visit to the Pope (which caused some trouble with Protestant feeling at home) the real diplomatic crisis of the tour loomed up; the King prepared for his journey on to France.

Although Cambon and Delcassé (the French Foreign Minister) had for some time been working quietly towards an understanding, and although the Accession envoy had been assured by President Loubet in 1901 that 'the immense popularity (of the King) in Paris would go a long way to smooth the path for this', feelings in France were still intensely anti-British. The memory of the Fashoda crisis was fresh and sections of French opinion seemed determined to keep it so. But Edward resisted attempts by French ministers to keep the visit discreetly unpublicised and he was met by Loubet in full state when he arrived at the Bois de Boulogne station on 1 May 1903. The gesture of sending a British squadron to salute the French President on his recent visit to Algiers had been greatly appreciated in official quarters but the drive to the British embassy from the station nevertheless turned into the most obvious demonstration the French people had made against British imperial policy for many years. Cries of 'Vive Fashoda!' and 'Vive les Boers!' and even 'Vive Jeanne d'Arc!' assailed the ears of the King. A more touchy ruler, such as the Kaiser, might have reacted disastrously, but Edward remained calm. 'The French don't like us', someone remarked, and he replied sensibly, 'Why should they?'

During the next few days he set himself out with great skill and patience to win the volatile sympathy of the Parisian population. In a speech, again written by Hardinge, to a

'The French don't like us'

160

deputation of the British Chamber of Commerce, Edward mentioned 'the days of conflict' between Britain and France as being 'happily over' and gave vent to the hope that 'England and France may be regarded as the champions and pioneers of peaceful progress and civilisation'. Echoing the Kaiser's ideas on the role of providence in fitting 'teutonic nations' for co-operation, Edward pointed out the physical nearness of Britain and France, and stated that the encouragement of 'affection and attachment' between the two peoples was his 'constant desire'. At a performance of *L'Autre Danger* (Edward had specified that he be shown a new play, and not a Molière classic, more fitted for the Shah of Persia) he complimented the actress, Mlle Granier, whom he met in the lobby during the interval, as 'representing all the grace and spirit of France'. These diverse remarks filtered into the evening papers. When the King drove to Vincennes the following day, the crowds, attracted by his evident good nature, were noticeably less hostile. After a speech from the Hôtel de Ville in which he stressed his links with and long affection for Paris, came the first signs of positive enthusiasm. A state banquet at the Elysée allowed an interchange of felicitous compliments between King and President, and on 4 May, when the King left for the station for his journey home, the crowd yelled, 'Vive notre Roi!'

'Vive notre Roi!'

The tour of 1903 was certainly Edward's most dramatic contribution to the shape of European diplomacy. The people of Paris and perhaps of France had broken for him the harsh front of the previous decade of hostility. The King's personal appearance in Paris, followed by the visit of Loubet and Delcassé to London, was of long-term importance and there was more than symbolic significance in the reception which each side received. The British ambassador in Paris noted the sudden growth of 'a feeling of gratification only equalled by the satisfaction of that large body of politicians who ... have always systematically favoured the *entente cordiale*'. Later, in 1908, Eyre Crowe, then Assistant Under-Secretary at the Foreign Office, noted in a memorandum circulated by Grey among the Cabinet, that the 'tactful perseverance' of the King in Paris had been the essential prelude for preparing public opinion on both sides of the Channel for the *entente*. Loubet, too, believed that

the visit had 'strengthened the bonds'; and a Belgian representative wrote that 'Edward VII has won the hearts of all the French. Seldom has such a complete change of attitude been seen as that which has taken place in this country during the last fortnight towards England.'

Of course it is true that the diplomatic and political climate in both countries favoured a *rapprochement*; also that, once the ice was broken, further detailed negotiation of the terms lay in the hands of Delcassé and Lansdowne. But the King was shown Lansdowne's preparatory draft for comment before it went to the Cabinet, and he was able to qualify it to remove references to Britain's annexation of Egypt and also to stress the necessity of safe-guarding commercial interests in Morocco. The treaty itself was a diplomatic construction, based on the adjustment of colonial differences, involving some exchanges of territory and the referring of some disputes to international arbitration. In some ways it was an insecure link, for its secret provisions did not rest on the support of public opinion. The existence of Anglo-French staff talks was kept hidden because the British public would not have approved of them any more than would

L'entente cordiale 1903.
Edward visited Paris and
was greeted with derisory
shouts, but his charm and
tact won the sympathy of
the French people.
OPPOSITE Edward is
cheered on his way to the
Gare du Bois de Boulogne,
at the end of his stay.
RIGHT *Punch* cartoon
showing the return visit
made by the French
President Loubet which
helped to create the
entente.

PUNCH, OR THE LONDON CHARIVARI

FRIENDS!

German opinion. But the King's blessing gave the *entente* a
launching which assured it the seal of popular approval. For
good or ill, he identified himself with the cause of Anglo-French
friendship and he added to the bare bones of the treaty an
element of national sympathy, which survived even though,
by the end of his reign, the French were having their doubts as
to its efficacy in protecting France in a war situation.

Repercussions to the *entente* varied: immediate reactions in
Germany were restrained. F. von Holstein, a high official in the
German Foreign Office, stressed that, 'although the Paris visit
cannot be considered a very friendly action with regard to
Germany, it is not likely to change the grouping of the powers,
which is dictated by force of circumstances and not by the
contributions of statesmen'. Although Germany greeted the
Anglo-French agreement with apparent unconcern, however,
the British ambassador in Berlin was asked if the King intended
to visit the Kaiser that year; and Edward's role in 1903 marked
the beginning of the movement of hostile opinion in Germany
from considering him merely as an ineffectual and corrupt
libertine towards a conception of him as a subtle Machiavelli,

constructing a diplomatic policy of encirclement aimed at the heart of Germany.

The King's tours of the Continent and his meetings with his fellow heads of State continued throughout his reign. There were several meetings with the Kaiser through official visits to Kiel in 1904 and Berlin in 1909, and unofficial meetings, usually *en route* for Marienbad: at Kronberg in 1906 and 1908, and Kassel in 1907. Other rulers were seen on State visits to Vienna (1903), Cartagena (Spain, 1907), and Reval (Russia, 1908). Also there were casual meetings with the Czar at the birthday celebrations of King Christian of Denmark in the early part of the reign, and similar unofficial encounters with Franz Joseph of Austria in Ischl in 1907 and 1908. To complete the circuit of Europe left uncovered in 1903, he made tours of the Mediterranean in 1905 and Greece in 1906, and an official tour of Scandinavian states in 1908. In return, Edward extended the hospitality of Britain on several occasions, the most important of which were the visits of the Kaiser to Windsor in 1907, the President of France in 1908, and the Czar of Russia in 1909. Minor royalty from Europe and Asia whom he entertained included the King of Siam, the Prince of Bulgaria and the boy-King Manuel of Portugal.

The British Government was aware of the potential value of these interchanges and the Foreign Office ensured that the King was fully briefed on British interests and the desirable attitudes to take. A minister plenipotentiary accompanied him on all his visits to take part in discussions with foreign officials and ministers. Balfour believed that the meeting with the Emperor William at Kiel 'must have a good effect upon international relations', and Haldane suggested that the Kronberg encounter in 1906 might 'inaugurate a period of facility and ease in interchange of views and this might prove very useful to the Foreign Office'. Sir Edward Grey, who succeeded Lansdowne as Foreign Secretary in 1905, considered the Mediterranean cruises valuable 'from a Foreign Office point of view'. The high point of the Foreign Office optimism about what Edward might accomplish was shown in the hopes Grey held out for the second Kronberg meeting in 1908, when the possibility of an Anglo-German naval agreement was in the air. In sending Edward a full memorandum on the British position, Grey

OPPOSITE Edward's difficult relations with his nephew, the German Kaiser, are shown in this German cartoon of 1909 – from the German viewpoint, of course. The angels of peace of Germany and England float above the figures of Edward and William (wearing a kilt as an ironical reference to his Scottish ancestry) arm-in-arm, in apparent accord. The caption reads: 'I would like to shake hands with you, but please take the boxing gloves off first!'

München, 8. Februar 1909

13. Jahrgang No.

SiMPLiCiSSiMUS

Herausgeber: Albert Langen

Abonnement vierteljährlich 3 Mk. 60 Pfg.

In Oesterreich-Ungarn vierteljährl. K

(Alle Rechte vorbehalten)

Der deutsche und der englische Friedensengel

(Th. Th. Heine)

„Ich möchte Ihnen ja gern die Hand geben. Aber wollen Sie nicht erst Ihre Boxhandschuhe ausziehen?"

indicated that great credit would rest with him and the Kaiser as peace-makers, 'if it could be shown that, as a result of the interview between the two sovereigns, a slackening of activity in the building programmes of the two navies had ensued'. Of course, it was up to the King to raise the issue, bearing in mind that the visit was an essentially private one, 'a personal matter between the King and the Emperor in which the King's own knowledge and judgement of the Emperor's disposition is much superior to any of us'. 'This was really a very interesting innovation', Hardinge commented, 'since for the first time in history, the British Government briefed the King to act as their spokesman ... it serves as an indisputable proof of the confidence they felt in the wisdom and tact of the sovereign in dealing with such matters.'

'The British Government briefed the King to act as their spokesman'

Such a direct call on the King was rare. Usually the important discussions took place between ministers and, whereas the King set the tone, the Foreign Office was aware of the valuable contribution made by Hardinge, who accompanied Edward on most of his tours and remained in constant communication with his superiors in London. It was not, after all, in the nature of the King's encounters with foreign sovereigns that they should lead immediately to agreements of precise detail. It was the King's task mainly to publicise the British case, not to solve intricate problems personally. Where information came to him through the royal network, he was quick to pass it on to the Foreign Office. The Czar, for example, wrote to him in 1901, in what was taken to be an expression of Russian hostility to the continuance of the Boer War; again, in 1904, the Czar sent a letter to Edward requesting that no other state should 'mix in this affair of ours in Japan [the Russo-Japanese War]'. Edward always consulted Lansdowne before sending a reply. In the latter case he wrote, indicating that Britain would remain out of the conflict unless the terms of peace were hostile to the established interests of other powers.

The most striking failure of the King's efforts to ease the obstacles in the way of British interests remained, throughout his reign, the overtures to Germany. Personal meetings with the Kaiser never produced much by way of concrete agreement. In 1907 the desire of the German Emperor to deal with the problem of the Baghdad railway terminal was frustrated because German diplomats wanted direct discussions, whereas the British Cabinet refused to open talks unless the Russians and French took part. During his visit to Britain, the Kaiser also spent much of the time describing to the King the iniquities of the Jews – a sentiment which was scarcely productive in diplomatic terms. At Kronberg in 1908, in spite of Grey's high hopes, Edward was unable to get an unwilling Kaiser to discuss the problem of Anglo-German naval rivalry, possibly because the subject was not one on which the King, influenced by Fisher and already worried at the decline of the British naval supremacy, was a particularly neutral party. On the other hand, the Foreign Office may well have been grateful for the King's tactful restraint. The experiences of other royal encounters in the pre-war period were not happy, the classic example being the meeting between the Czar and the Kaiser at Björkö in 1905, where the Czar was cajoled into signing a treaty which would have contravened Russia's commitments to France. In the event, his ministers, with much embarrassment, were forced to repudiate it.

Gestures Edward's tours might be, but apart from his conquest of Paris in 1903, initiatives in policy-making they were not. Thus, in 1906, the King and his staff rejected the idea of a State visit to Russia because the terms of the Anglo-Russian agreement had not then been reached, and relations were still uneasy. The King's visit to Reval in 1908 was valuable, not because it opened up channels of communication with the Russian Empire, but because it added the crowning touch to the *entente* that had been signed; it came after the diplomats had done their work and gave a lead, in the words of the *National Review*, to 'every patriotic Englishman to co-operate'.

How close then were the King and the policy-makers? Was it true, as suspicious foreign observers, notably the Kaiser in his more extreme moments of Anglophobia, imagined, that the visits to Austria and Italy were intended to detach these countries from the Triple Alliance; or that the tours of the Mediterranean, Scandinavia and Russia formed part of a deep design to encircle Germany on the part of the British Government? Did they misunderstand the nature of the King's link with his ministers?

Primed with similar information by the Foreign Office, there was little likelihood that King and Cabinet would draw widely differing conclusions. The presence of Hardinge on the King's staff on foreign tours ensured close co-ordination with London, and it is noticeable that the King reacted strongly against the pro-German views expressed by the more radical members of the Liberal Cabinet. There were some differences of opinion during the reign, but on minor matters, such as the desirability of union between Crete and Greece, and the King always bowed to the Government's wishes. In 1902 he urged Lansdowne to emphasise to the Sultan the need to ameliorate the condition of his Christian subjects in Macedonia – if necessary by 'a naval demonstration' – but he withdrew the suggestions when Lansdowne pointed out the risks of unilateral action.

Insiders tended to overrate the King's part, understandably enough. Ponsonby explained the quarrel between the King and Lansdowne over the Shah of Persia's Garter as stemming from the Foreign Secretary's jealousy 'at the King being supposed to run the foreign policy of this country'. The opposite could equally well have been true. Their lack of mutual understanding was due probably more to the British predicament at the time, which gave no satisfaction to anyone concerned with national prestige. With Grey the King was usually in complete accord, although it took Mrs Keppel to persuade him that Lloyd George and Churchill were imperialists at heart, despite their unwelcome incursions into foreign policy. Once, towards the end of the reign, he took offence when the Foreign Office asked him to meet the Kaiser, after the latter had given an interview to the *New York World* in which he spoke of Edward as a corrupt monarch at the head of a corrupt court. This was all the more galling since it followed the Kaiser's State visit to Britain, but although Edward complained to Knollys that 'the Foreign Office, to gain their own object will not care a pin what humiliation I have to put up with', he consented.

There were also some difficulties because of the King's social predilections. He disliked receiving the Turkish ambassador, whose past was somewhat chequered, referring to his unwillingness to turn his residence into 'a refuge for disreputable Levantines'. Also, his hatred of boredom led to a refusal to entertain South American diplomats.

In following up the consequences of the Anglo-French *entente*, Edward was able to offer his complete and whole-

'They will not care a pin what humiliation I have to put up with'

hearted support to the policy of the Foreign Office. The next step was to come to a similar agreement with Russia; and during the course of the Russo-Japanese War, the King wrote to Czar Nicholas, stressing his earnest desire 'that at the conclusion of the war our two countries may come to a satisfactory settlement ... similar to the one which we have lately concluded with France'. In October 1904 the Russian Baltic fleet, on its way to attack the Japanese in the Pacific, shelled some British trawlers in the Channel under the impression that they were Japanese vessels, and the incident threatened to get out of hand. Edward reacted vigorously: 'The Russian admiral *must* be punished for his conduct ... public opinion is running very high and something must be done to appease it.' But after receiving Admiral Rozdestvensky's report, and having considered the implications for Anglo-Russian relations, Edward reconsidered and wrote to Lansdowne to ask, 'Are we prepared to go to war with her ... all for the sake of the heirs of two harmless fishermen?' Despite the difficulties caused by this affair and the numerous barriers on the way to Anglo-Russian agreement (Britain was already linked with Japan through the Alliances of 1902 and 1905; many leading Russians looked to Germany for the protection of Russian interests in Asia after the war; and British Liberals who tended to sympathise with the opposition, were outraged when Nicholas dissolved the Duma, or Parliament, in 1905), Edward gave his support to Hardinge and others in the Foreign Office who were working towards an extension of the *entente* to cover Russo-British interests in Persia. Co-operation over the Morocco question and the failure of the German diplomatic offensive at Björkö helped, and the King was glad to hear that in September 1907 the Convention had been signed by Nicholson, British ambassador in St Petersburg, and Isvolsky.

'Are we prepared to go to war ...?'

The King's part was not inconsiderable, for although the Anglo-Russian agreement was not in any sense a major treaty between the two countries, it served to break the ice that for many years had encrusted Anglo-Russian relations. Among the personal factors involved was the King's friendship with Sir Donald Wallace, *The Times* expert on Russian affairs, and with Isvolsky himself, for whom he had considerable respect. Later, and most unusually, when the Russian Foreign Minister's position weakened after the Austrian annexation of Bosnia-

169

One of the causes of the difficulties between Edward and the Kaiser was the Anglo-Japanese alliances of 1902 and 1905. This cartoon from *Le Rire* shows the Japanese Emperor with Edward and alludes to the alliance: 'European diplomacy has produced another Siamese twin'.

Herzogovina, Edward wrote to the Czar to back him up: 'You know how anxious I am for the most friendly relations between Russia and England, not only in Asia but also in Europe, and I feel confident that through M. Isvolsky these hopes will be realised.'

All the King's enthusiasm for France and the French was needed to sustain the policy of the *entente* through the difficult years of 1905–7, when it seemed to lead into head-on conflict with Germany. At the instance of the German Foreign Office, the Kaiser went to Tangier in 1905, where he made speeches declaring German interest in the future of Morocco, thus aiming a blow at further encroachment by France on the sovereignty of the Sultan. With German backing, the Sultan then suggested a conference of the major powers to discuss the future of his country and the control of the open ports where foreign trade was concentrated. This interference in what had been recognised as a French sphere of influence by the Anglo-French agreement, was at once repudiated by Delcassé who refused to attend the proposed conference. Under threat of war from Germany, however, (and pressure from the United States) the French were forced to reconsider and eventually to replace the anti-German Delcassé himself. It appeared a great victory for the new style of German diplomacy. The British were astounded and reacted strongly: 'These annual cruises of the Kaiser', Edward wrote to Lansdowne, 'are deeply to be deplored and mischief is their only object.' During the period before the conference met at Algeciras, he gave his support to gestures of solidarity with France. The British fleet visited Brest and the French admiral of the squadron which returned the visit at Portsmouth was entertained by the King himself. Just before the conference met, Edward expressed to Cambon the position of the British Government: 'Tell us what you wish on each point and we will support you without restriction and reserve.'

His efforts were successful; the conference proved a severe disappointment for German hopes. Since the British and Russians were backing the French demands and Italy seemed willing to fulfill her obligations to the Triple Alliance, the United States, which had been instrumental in forcing the French to the conference table, also supported resolutions acceptable to French opinion. Germany was left isolated and unable to secure a part in the Franco–Spanish police force set up to control the ports. By co-operating with Spain, France was able to continue her economic penetration of Morocco, benefiting from the overthrow of the Sultan in 1907 by a rival to the throne. The main plank of the *entente*, the agreements on Morocco and Egypt, survived intact. To continue the policy of the *entente* and to co-operate (as far as British interests permitted) with France in European questions became as a result a leading principle of British diplomacy and one to which the King gave full backing.

In later years, when Edward passed through Paris, he always contrived to meet the French President, and a private meeting with Clemenceau at Marienbad in 1907 was particularly valuable. As Sir Edward Grey wrote: 'The moment being specially opportune after your Majesty's interview with the two Emperors [the King had visited the Kaiser and Franz Joseph that year], it has given great satisfaction in France.' In 1908

Edward entertained President Fallières at the Anglo-French Exhibition and, although he commented somewhat testily that there was 'some danger of the *entente cordiale* being worn bare if these demonstrations are overdone', the visit was extremely cordial. All this contributed to the fact that, after his death, Edward's name was linked firmly with the *entente* policy. It is worth remembering two points, however. The policy was not simply a personal creation, but the response of British diplomacy to the problem of isolation among the Continental powers, and it was designed primarily to relieve Britain's difficulties in her colonies and other areas, mainly in Africa, where the major powers seemed likely to get embroiled. Secondly, the ties with France and Russia were not as rigid as many, including the Kaiser, believed. In 1914 Britain went to war as much because of the violation of Belgian neutrality and the immediate threat to the balance of power, as because of her commitments to the Dual Alliance. Although one of the founders of the *entente*, Edward was not the architect of 1914.

Yet this was precisely the charge levelled against him by some German observers in the first year of the war, notably by Reinhold Wagner, the author of a pamphlet called, *Edward VII of England: The Greatest Criminal Against Humanity in the Twentieth Century*. It is crucial to realise that, whatever the aims of British policy were and whatever the part the King took in making it, the *impression* given to foreign statesmen could be as important as the reality. Nowhere was this more significant than in Anglo-German relations, where the All-Highest played a dynamic role in his country's foreign policy and was inclined to regard his uncle as playing an equally important part in Britain. German statesmen were obsessed by the fear of encirclement, by the threat of French revanchist demands for the return of Alsace-Lorraine (lost after the Franco-Prussian war), combined with Russian desires for Balkan expansion, and both backed up with the force of the British navy. Unreal though the fear was, the feeling of insecurity involved Germany in a series of incidents designed to break up the *entente* powers and led her government into the race for naval supremacy. After Algeciras, the image of Edward as an intriguer, even the leader of the encirclement policy, began to grow and was shared by other more sober judges than the Kaiser. As late as February 1905, Baron Greindl,

'The Greatest Criminal Against Humanity'

Belgian representative in Berlin, could consider Edward as a potential friend of Germany. 'Edward VII is said to be a whole-hearted lover of peace, but the King of England has only a very limited influence in shaping the course of his country's politics,' he wrote. This sensible verdict was modified sharply after the King had shown sympathy with Delcassé and the French demands at Algeciras. In April 1906 the Baron commented: 'One is driven to the conclusion that English foreign policy is directed by the King in person ... there is undoubtedly in England a court policy pursued outside and alongside that of the responsible Government.'

During 1905, when they were constantly in correspondence, the Kaiser was offended by the British attitude over Morocco and the Czar by the ties of Britain with Japan. Consequently, British foreign policy, personified by the King, came in for harsh criticism. The incidents noted by the Kaiser may have appeared trivial (Edward's failure to visit him on his way to Marienbad in that year, and so on) but they reflected the tension. The Czar referred to the King as 'the greatest mischief-maker and the most deceitful and dangerous intriguer in the world', and William enthusiastically confirmed this caricature of his uncle. The Björkö meeting between them was, in part, a personal gesture of defiance against Edward, and the Kaiser revelled in the fact that his uncle was worried and ignorant about what had taken place there.

Was it possible for Edward to have dispelled this illusion? After all, the Björkö and Moroccan initiatives failed. As the German naval programme was speeded up, as the Berlin-Baghdad railway extended German influence in Turkey, and as the signs of an Anglo-Russian *rapprochement* became evident, there were valid reasons for a breach in Anglo-German relations that went far beyond the personal antipathies of their monarchs. In any case, the antipathies were real. Edward did find the company of his nephew very trying and was always concerned that the Kaiser might 'spring some new surprise' on him. Equally, William refused to place any reliance on Edward's professions of peace 'because he is envious'. The King's visits to Spain and Italy in 1907 inspired new suspicions of encirclement, and Baron Greindl reflected: 'The King of England's visit to the King of Spain is one of the moves in the campaign to isolate

'English foreign policy is directed by the King in person'

173

At the beginning of the First World War, many Germans looked back upon Edward as the architect of the catastrophe. This fierce cartoon by Adolph Hengler of Munich, appeared in 1914, and depicts Edward the Sower, followed by Death the Reaper.

Germany that is being personally directed … by His Majesty King Edward VII.' At a dinner given by the Knights of St John in 1907, the Kaiser complained that 'the whole press of the world' was being 'mobilised against him by British money'. Edward was 'a Satan, you can hardly believe what a Satan he is'.

In both countries the press whipped up feeling: the *Neue Freie Presse* asked its readers, 'What is the meaning of this continual political labour carried on with open recklessness?' and provided the answer: 'To put a close ring round Germany.' Although the King had made some efforts to restrain the virulently anti-German tone of *The Times*, contact between the two rulers remained edgy. Ponsonby observed that 'there was always electricity in the air' when they met. Given William's flamboyant manner and his habit of making provocative gestures, as in announcing an extension of the German navy the day after the State visit to Windsor ended in 1907, it was not surprising. The Kaiser personally believed that Edward was out to bring Germany down. He commented on a minute from the German ambassador in London that, far from desiring peace, the British monarch 'aims at war'. He traced Edward's hand in every diplomatic event in any way hostile to Germany's interests – even the *nem con* declaration in 1908 by Ferdinand of Bulgaria that his state was totally independent of Turkey. No

Despite their mutual suspicion and distrust, the Kaiser and Edward continued to visit each other. This photograph was taken on the State visit of Edward to Berlin in February 1909.

doubt the resentment felt by William had some psychological foundation, but these clashes of personality reflected and added to the diplomatic obstacles to Anglo-German understanding.

One should not forget the consistently anti-German influence on the King emphasised by Queen Alexandra, who in 1903 was still vividly recounting the sufferings of the Danes in Schleswig-Holstein. Entertaining or visiting the Kaiser was a particular strain on the Queen.

The final diplomatic crisis of Edward's reign demonstrated the inherent dangers of these royal encounters. In 1908 the King made what seemed to be an innocuous visit to the Austrian Emperor at Ischl. Hardinge had useful conversations with Aerenthal on the Balkan situation, where the Young Turk Party seemed to be moving towards power in Constantinople. Some weeks later, however, the journalist Wickham Steed told Edward that the Austrians intended to annex the territory of Bosnia-Herzogovina (which they had administered since 1878 under the terms of the Treaty of Berlin, but which remained in theory part of the Turkish Empire). This the King refused to believe: 'The Emperor Franz Joseph gave me no hint of anything of the sort. No, I cannot believe that ... surely the Emperor would have said something to me.' A few days later, news came through that the annexation had taken place and Edward's reaction was one of absolute fury. Accusing the Austrian Government of lying to him, he refused ever to meet Franz Joseph again (although he did return to Marienbad – there were things above politics). In 1909 he referred to Aerenthal as 'almost the Devil Incarnate'.

The affair also revealed the royal limitations. While Serbia and Russia demanded compensation and Germany and Austria resisted it, the King had to leave the conduct of British policy to the Cabinet. British diplomats paid scant regard to his efforts to secure meaningful concessions to Russia in the Dardanelles and Asquith did not over-value the King's suggestions that the terms of the 1909 Budget should be considered in relation to 'the possible (but the King hopes unlikely) event of a European war'. The crisis left Serbia and Russia resentful at Austrian success and it illustrates how far Britain had progressed among the Continental powers since 1901. Unbound by firm commitments on the Continent itself, Britain benefited from the machinery for settling colonial disputes with Russia and France. At the same time, the aggressive policy of the Triple Alliance diminished the prospect of a Continental union against her. European stability, however, had not been achieved.

The King's presence was a substantial asset to British diplomacy. His manner created a good impression abroad and contrasted favourably with the arrogant antics of the Kaiser. In 1903 the Emperors of Russia and Germany and the King of England passed through Vienna in rapid succession. *Die Zeit* noted the contrast between them – the military pomp of the Kaiser, the underhand secrecy and caution of the Czar, and the open friendliness of the King. 'The Englishman', it concluded, 'is free and without fear of his King and the King is free and ... was not afraid of the Viennese.' Of the royal visit, Sir Harold Nicolson wrote: 'The Czar had returned from Björkö and Swinemunde frightened and humiliated. The greatest diplomatic victories are gained by doing nothing; and King Edward, although too superficial to be a statesman, was a supreme diplomatist.' True, he precipitated a minor political crisis at home, when he made the Czar an Admiral of the British fleet in 1908, but on the credit side there was much to be said for small gestures, such as getting *The Mikado* taken off the London

OPPOSITE The savage comment of the French newspaper *Le Rire* on Edward's accession to the throne. It refers back to Edward's great-uncle, George IV, whose dissolute and extravagant habits first as Prince of Wales, and then as King, had made him such an unpopular monarch. To many in 1901, it seemed that George IV had come again to the throne of England.

176

N° 326. 7e année. 2 Février 1901.   15 centimes.

Le Rire

JOURNAL HUMORISTIQUE PARAISSANT LE SAMEDI

an : Paris, 8 fr.   122, rue Réaumur, 122
nts, 9 fr. Étranger, 12 fr.   M. Félix JUVEN, Directeur. — Partie artistique : M. Arsène ALEXANDRE   PARIS
France, 5 fr. Étranger, 650   La reproduction des dessins du RIRE est absolument interdite aux publications, françaises ou étrangères, sans autorisation   Vente et Abonnement
                                                                                                             9, rue Saint-Joseph, 9

LE GOTHA DU « RIRE ». — N° XXXIII   ÉDOUARD VII, roi d'Angleterre, empereur des Indes

(Air connu.)   Et ta mère à son oncle,
Edouard-Albert,   Qu'était roi d'Angleterre !
Tu succèd' à ta mère.

stage during the visit of a Japanese diplomat in 1907. In his refusal to have anything to do with King Leopold because of the atrocious Belgian policy in the Congo, Edward was in line with the demands of both public opinion and his Government. Certainly there was a world of difference between his methods and those of the Kaiser, who was inclined to make an appeal to the British public, starting off, 'You British are mad, mad as March hares'. He would never have dreamed of giving a *Daily Telegraph* interview, as the Kaiser did, with disastrous effect in 1908, and for this the Foreign Office might have been sincerely grateful.

There were those, like Monsieur Cartier, the Belgian Chargé d'Affaires in London, who thought that 'the English are getting more and more in the habit of regarding international problems as being almost exclusively within the province of King Edward'. Even political realists, like Stolypin, the Russian Prime Minister, could say: 'It is not only what he said [at Reval in 1908] but his manner that bore the impression of an artist in international affairs, whom Europe regarded as the first statesmen in Europe.' But Edward's role in the development of British foreign policy was supportive rather than formative. By 1909 even the comptroller of the Kaiser's household realised that 'the part he plays in the affairs of his country is smaller than we have imagined'. At the end of his reign Edward was prepared to admit the limitations. In March 1909 he wrote to Hardinge: 'It is strange that ever since my visit to Berlin, the German Government have done *nothing* but thwart and annoy us in every way … if only we can ensure peace it is worth giving way, as long as we can do so with honour and dignity.' By temperament the King was certainly not a Kaiser William II.

The maintenance of Britain's interests, in conformity with his Government's plans was Edward's lifelong aim. In so far as he can be said to have had a consistent principle beyond this, it was a basic sympathy with the institution of monarchy. He refused to have any dealings with the Serbian Government that overthrew King Alexander in 1903, until the successor of the rival house of Karageorgevich had placed the regicide officers on the retired list. In Norway, Portugal and Greece, he supported the monarchical system, suggesting (but not insisting upon) a naval and military demonstration to protect Manuel of Portugal, when the young ruler was threatened in 1908 by the forces which had assassinated his father. In 1906, after an attempt on the life of King Alfonso of Spain, Edward wrote to the Czar concerning 'the difficulty to cope with the pest of mankind, as you rightly observe, that in some countries – before all in England – these beasts may live undisturbed and there plot against the lives of anybody'.

In the course of his own peregrinations, Edward faced the same threat. He did not hesitate to pass through Paris in 1907 and 1908 when the city was torn by strikes. 'It would be interesting to see a revolution', he remarked somewhat patronisingly. Nevertheless, during the 1903 tour the Foreign Office ensured that an eye was kept on the movements of any suspicious character near the King, and the danger of assassination explains why it was thought advisable to conduct the visits to Spain and Russia from aboard ship. At Reval, when a boat came alongside bearing a choir which serenaded the King and the Emperor, the British party were assured that all the singers had been stripped and searched before being allowed in such close proximity.

There was a feeling that, in some way, King Edward stood for peace. There was a popular song in the repertoire of Pelissier's Follies in 1909:

> There'll be no wo'ar
> As long as there's a King like good King Edward.
> There'll be no wo'ar
> For 'e 'ates that sort of thing!
> ... Peace with 'Onner
> Is his Motter.
> So God Sive the King!

Edward believed that the peace of Europe *ought* to be preserved, but he was no pacifist. Towards the end of his reign he noted privately that 'if he [the Kaiser] goes on in that way [refusing to come to a naval agreement] a conflict between us and Germany is only a matter of time'. It is not unreasonable to suggest that he would have supported the action of the Government in declaring war on 4 August 1914.

King Edward was sovereign also of an Empire, yet it took up curiously little of his life, and much less of his devotion than it had of Queen Victoria's. His mature judgement derived more

LEFT Cartoon on the 1909 Budget.

BELOW The Conservatives counter the Liberal attack by claiming that free trade will depress home industry and workers will have no money to buy imported goods.

from the attitudes of the 1870s, before Disraeli made India the 'brightest jewel' in the imperial diadem, and Edward always saw colonial affairs through European eyes. The Empire was something to be preserved rather than extended after the South African War, and its protection, he believed, was best secured by agreements with France and Russia and by the virtues of a firm administration. He did not visit any colonies personally during his reign, preferring to send the Prince of Wales or other members of the royal family to attend functions in India and Canada; and he raised some objection to the length of the Prince of Wales's tour of Canada and Australia in 1901–2. Although he showed an interest in the Younghusband expedition to Tibet and the progress towards federation in South Africa, his influence was cast in favour of the *status quo*. He expressed great objections to the Morley-Minto reform programme in India, but was powerless to reverse the decision of the Cabinet that native members should be admitted to the Viceroy's Council. In 1909 the King wrote to Morley that 'he could not change his views on this subject ... this proposed step is fraught with the greatest danger to the maintenance of the Indian Empire under British rule ...'. India remained for him the India of the Princes, and a problem in Anglo-Russian relations – to the new currents of unrest on the sub-continent he was totally unsympathetic. In South African affairs, the King was sometimes equally reactionary, standing out in favour of continuing to employ Chinese labour in the Transvaal and doubting the wisdom of giving responsible government to the defeated Boer provinces. But when good relations had been established between General Botha, the ex-Boer commander, and the British administration, and the Liberal policy had proved successful, the King was pleased to accept the gift of the Cullinan diamond from the Transvaal Legislative Assembly in 1907 – though he still made it clear that acceptance of this massive jewel was 'on the recommendation of the Cabinet'. Colonial administration he considered a matter purely for the Cabinet, except where personalities were involved. Thus he objected to Herbert Gladstone as High Commissioner for South Africa and he tried (unsuccessfully) to patch up the quarrel between Lord Curzon and Kitchener, which led eventually to Curzon's resignation as Viceroy of India. Lord

Cromer's administration in Egypt was much appreciated because he had gone far to mollify French interests and Edward urged him not to retire in 1907. When the ageing proconsul insisted, the King used his influence to see that a grant of money was made by the Government. Elsewhere, though well enough informed on colonial affairs and possessed of a lively sense of the value of Britain's overseas possessions, the King respected the ultimate authority of the Colonial Secretary and the Cabinet and did not get involved.

Looking back from the end of the reign in 1910, the European orientation of the King's mind becomes clear. His approach was traditional and bounded by arguments familiar fifty years before. He had no understanding of economics and would have been baffled if he had read Lenin's tract *Imperialism, the Highest*

Durbah 1903, the state entry of the Viceroy, Lord Curzon, into Delhi – in all his imperial glory. This was the heyday of the Indian Raj.

Stage of Capitalism. The strategic realities of trade and investment, the latent power of the United States fell outside his calculations. In this, however, he was scarcely more naïve than the statesmen of Europe, who invested the comings and goings of sovereigns with a mystique which was, in itself, a factor in diplomatic calculations. At a time when Britain's position among the European powers forced her external policy into new channels, King Edward's greatest personal contribution lay in what he did for the Anglo-French *entente* and in his willingness to work in co-operation with his ministers. In moving Britain away from 'splendid isolation' towards involvement in the currents of European diplomacy, it was of value to have a king whose contacts with the Continent were already developed when he came to the throne. In foreign affairs King Edward served his country well.

183

7
The King
in Society
1901-10

King Edward and his
party watch from
the royal stand as his
horse Minoru wins the
1909 Derby.

To IMAGINE KING EDWARD simply as the mirror of his age, its politics and diplomacy, is to fall into the same error as contemporary newspapers which captioned a picture of the King talking to Campbell-Bannerman in Marienbad with the words, 'Is it peace or war?' when they were in fact, as Campbell-Bannerman later revealed, discussing whether halibut was better boiled or baked. Journalists then, and historians since, have found it a great convenience to link his name with the characteristics of the thirteen years between the death of Queen Victoria and the outbreak of the First World War; but this habit in some ways misplaces the King's own predilections. His character, friendships and style of life had determined, long before his accession, that his career would not simply be one of administration, but also one of pleasure. Having fought off boredom with the delights of hedonism during the years as Prince of Wales, Edward never slackened the pursuit as King. But as time passed and he grew older, his pleasures became more sedentary and acquired an aspect of grossness, unpleasing to the modern eye. Having been in many ways a modern figure in contrast to Queen Victoria, he later became isolated through the formal structure of the court. He revelled in the sphere of banquets and country house parties, but knew little of the changes in the world many stages beneath, catalogued in the horrifying contemporary surveys of Booth and Seebohm Rowntree.

Not for centuries, since the royal progresses of Queen Elizabeth I, had the monarch travelled so widely and continuously as Edward VII. The opening months of the year would see him at the State Opening of Parliament; in the spring he would be off for a visit to Biarritz, with a short stop in Paris on the way. In April there was the annual – and rather dreary – pilgrimage to Denmark to his father-in-law's austere court, and then the welcome relief of Epsom for Derby week, followed by Ascot. In July and August Edward would enjoy the hospitality of his friends at home and attend Cowes for the yachting week. During September and October he would travel to Marienbad (Homburg fell out of favour after one visit early in the reign) when he took the 'cure' of mineral water and mild exercise in the company of the aristocracy of Europe. Then there was the autumn shooting at Balmoral, and Christmas at Windsor, or

Edward loved to attend the Regatta week in Cowes in July.
ABOVE Cowes Regatta, 1909. The royal yacht is just left of the centre.
RIGHT The King's racing yacht, the *Britannia*.

Sandringham. What little time remained was spent in London, where he entertained and gave formal receptions at Marlborough House and Buckingham Palace or stayed in the houses of his friends within easy reach of London – Lord Crewe, Lord Carrington, Lord Rosebery, Lord Iveagh, Lord Londonderry, the Gurneys, Harcourts and Sassoons, to name but a few.

The house where the King chose to stay had to accommodate his retinue (sixteen if he were alone and twenty-two if the Queen accompanied him) and the host and his wife had to prepare a good deal more than mere stately comfort. Above all Edward feared boredom and idleness – his time had continually to be filled by conversation and games or hunting, as well as palatial meals. The only host whose dullness was immune from instant ostracism was the Danish King, and, as his staff knew,

OPPOSITE Edward VII in his full majesty as King and Emperor. A portrait by Sir Luke Fildes.

Edward found the Copenhagen court particularly trying. Those who had the charmed ability to keep the King amused were always in demand, hence the inclusion of Mrs Keppel or Louise de Soveral at many country house parties. For those who lacked the gift, the ordeal was frightening: one can sympathise with the lady who desperately asked Frederick Ponsonby what on earth she could talk to the King about at dinner, after three evenings of sitting next to him. The drumming of fingers on the table, the mutterings of 'Quite so, quite so', were signs which struck terror in the heart of many a hostess. Nonetheless, the royal tastes were simple enough and witty remarks and practical jokes could usually be relied upon. Even the outbursts of royal temper, terrible though they were and seldom forgotten by the recipient, were short-lived. As Ponsonby noted: 'It was usual with the King, after he had let himself go and cursed someone, to smooth matters by being especially nice to them afterwards.'

The social circle of Edward's close friends changed very little after 1901. The plutocracy remained in favour: the King became godfather to Sir Ernest Cassel's daughter (who was later to marry the future Lord Mountbatten) and he still sailed with Sir Thomas Lipton. Indeed, on board *Shamrock II* Edward broke his knee-cap in an accident that might have been fatal. Elegant foreign diplomats such as Soveral and Count Mensdorff, Austrian ambassador in London, were as acceptable as English aristocrats. Chatsworth, seat of the Duke of Devonshire, was a particularly favoured haunt and the King stayed there regularly each January from 1904 to 1907. A typically successful entertainment took place at Chatsworth in 1907, when the observant Ponsonby recorded evening theatricals, graced by the singing of Lady Maude Warrender and Princess Daisy of Pless, and a dinner on the Twelfth Night of Christmas when the fun was 'fast and furious' and Arthur Balfour appeared wearing a paper hat. On this occasion Edward told Ponsonby, on the third night of the party, that he intended to invest the Duke with the GCVO as a token of his favour.

Scarcely any country house was complete without its shooting party. The King liked 'masses of pheasants driven over his head, about the height of an ordinary tree' so that 'he never seemed to miss; but', Ponsonby added, 'he never shot at a

difficult bird'. The royal vanity was carefully maintained: beaters always made sure that the quarry was driven in the King's direction, although on one occasion when he shot at the estate of the monastery of Tepl, near Marienbad, the King found the arrangements sadly lacking and the bag was low. Shooting and hunting were sports common among the fashionable aristocracy of Europe and, although the King was never as good a shot as his son, George v, he could certainly hold his own among his friends. Their jokes revolved around it. The King was tireless in ribbing Sir Felix Semon for shooting a stag below the minimum weight at Balmoral in 1903, and when the unfortunate guest caught a fifteen-pound salmon, asked cuttingly, 'Did it have horns?' It relieved what might otherwise have been an unbearingly boring social occasion. It was also a sport confined to the very wealthy. Over four hundred beaters were employed in Prince Trautmansdorff's shoots with the King at Marienbad. The photographs of the period show the party standing by great heaps of game, and in the course of the King's life his bag included bear, chamois, big game, crocodile, deer, elk, grouse, partridge, pheasant and wild boar. Some of the shooting parties were enormous and in 1894 at Baron Hirsch's estate in Austria, he was present at the largest shoot ever held in Europe. Records were made even in England: a rabbit shoot on the Wynard estate of Lord Londonderry yielded three thousand on the first day alone. Edward seems never to have tired of the exercise of his skill with the gun, and a more modern taste, offended perhaps by the continuous mass slaughter, may conclude that there were more dangerous means available before 1914 for monarchs to work off their feelings of aggression.

More sedentary and harmless was the King's predilection for cards. The old days of baccarat were over – although the Queen enjoyed a version, played for low stakes, called Lotto – and during the reign his favourite game was bridge. He was a keen, if mediocre, player, who was inclined to place the blame for poor hands on his partners rather than himself. (He once bluntly told his partner, the King of Sweden, that a hand would have been won if only he had played out the cards; and on one occasion Mrs Keppel delighted him when she faced an almost impossible bid on poor cards by crying out, 'God save the King

TOP One of Edward's favourite amusements was shooting, and country house parties had to include opportunities to show royal prowess. He is shown here with his beaters at Sandringham, November 1908.

ABOVE Edward was also a keen motorist. This photograph depicts the first journey Edward made by car – in 1899. The car was an 1899 Daimler, 12 horse power, owned by Lord Montague of Beaulieu, here seen with Edward.

ABOVE Alexandra playing cards with her Danish parents Christian IX and the Empress Dagmar, and the Duchess of Cumberland.

Edward and the Theatre

Edward enjoyed visiting the theatre as both Prince and King. During his life many new theatres were built in London, and melodramas and musical variety performances became popular entertainment for all classes of society.

ABOVE The London
Hippodrome in 1902
painted by Everett Shinn.
The music hall was a very
popular form of
entertainment in
Edwardian England.
LEFT Edward and his party
in their extemporised
royal box in the pit of
the Drury Lane Theatre
in 1909.

OPPOSITE PAGE:
LEFT Mucha's poster
of Sarah Bernhardt in
Medée for the Théâtre de
la Renaissance in Paris.
RIGHT Two theatre
posters from the first
decade of the twentieth
century, advertising the
melodramas which had
become so popular.

193

and preserve Mrs Keppel!') Cards filled in the long evenings after dinner, for the King was growing rather old for dancing, and on foreign travels even reluctant and indifferent players were roped in to provide a four. During the Mediterranean cruise in 1905, John Ward and Frederick Ponsonby had to conspire to save the skin of Lord Salisbury, a bad bridge player and a worse partner for the King. At all games Edward took competition seriously, even croquet, as the Duchess of Sermoneta found out when a lucky shot of hers passed through her own hoop and then knocked the King's ball right out of the playing area into the nearby rose-bed. 'By the icy stillness that prevailed', she wrote later, 'I realised that never, never was such a thing to happen again.'

Although, as Ponsonby wrote, 'nature had not made his figure suitable for driving a long ball', the King took a lively interest in golf and ordered courses to be constructed at Sandringham and Windsor – a far cry from Albert's road-building and landscaping. Unfortunate shots tended to elicit the reaction, 'What a silly place to build a bunker! See that this is altered tomorrow' – and the golf course architect was kept busy moving obstacles to suit the royal temperament. Although he may not have been a skilled player, Edward was genuinely interested in this newly popular sport and he invited star players and professionals to perform on the royal courses. Even ice sports were not beyond his range and, as long as his health permitted, he was regularly out on the froken lakes of Sandringham in the winter, skating, and nominally keeping goal in ice hockey matches.

The royal interest in racing, however, was what caught the public fancy. No horses ran in the royal colours in 1901 because of court mourning for Queen Victoria, but the stable was kept up, managed by Marcus Beresford and trained by Richard Marsh. The King was not notably successful until 1909, when twenty-three horses were in the string and Minoru, bought for the stable in 1906, showed promising form. Entered for the Derby in that year, Minoru was a fancied runner and he came home at four to one. The scenes that followed were remarkable for the enthusiasm of the crowds. The King was mobbed as he led in the winner – the first Derby success for a racing monarch – and the crowd roared, 'Good Old Teddy!' and sang 'God Save the King'. Edward was most moved by the reception. In this one year he came second in the order of winning owners, with a total of £20,144 – a fitting climax to a long career of involvement in the affairs of the turf. How popular it made him is hard to judge: after his death Sir Edward Grey wrote that 'the humblest devotees of horse racing in a Derby day crowd knew that King Edward was there to enjoy the national festival in precisely the same spirit as themselves ... There was, in fact, a real sympathy and community of feeling between himself and his people'. His enthusiasm certainly endeared him to the frequenters of Newmarket and Epsom and compared favourably with the moral exclusiveness and rectitude of his mother and father, but while the sight of the old King leading in Minoru with obvious pride inspired affection, it came from those who already regarded the monarchy with devotion. Even on this occasion a few partisan cries were heard: 'Now, King, you've won the Derby. Go home and dissolve this bloody Parliament.'

'Now, King, you've won the Derby'

Almost as keen an interest of the King, and as far from the resources of the ordinary man as the ownership of race horses, was motoring; even the King's staff had to protest when a bill was submitted for £1,500 for a car Ponsonby had hired for the King in Marienbad one year. In 1899, when it could still be described as a sport for the adventurous, the then Prince of Wales had made his first journey in a Daimler belonging to Lord Montagu of Beaulieu. Shortly after the coronation he began to buy his own cars, including a Mercedes and a Renault, both painted a rich claret, and distinguished by their lack of number plates. Royal patronage was granted to the automobile exhibitions of 1903 and 1906, and the title 'Royal' to the Automobile Club. All his travelling in Ireland in 1907 was done by car and there were always limousines in attendance at Marienbad and Biarritz, but despite his love of motoring, the King remained lamentably ignorant of the workings of the internal combustion engine and he once found himself unable to tell the Kaiser what fuel the royal cars used. (The Kaiser's own suggestion of potato spirit rather than petrol was scarcely more enlightened.) A mechanic regularly accompanied the royal chauffeurs and the King's efforts were limited to urging his driver to overtake all the cars in front of him. Disregarding the

Court society under
Edward became glittering
and fashionable.
ABOVE Edward was very
interested in questions of
fashion, both for men and
for women. This is one of
the designs of Paquin for
September 1901 showing
une robe d'après-midi.
RIGHT A social gathering
of the early 1900s – the
emphasis is upon formality
and fashionable dress.

absurd speed limits of the day, on the Brighton road in 1906 they reached the heady maximum of 60 m.p.h. The sense of adventure was what Edward relished and he was courageous enough on one occasion to take his car right up to the top of the mountains in Majorca, when others in the royal party had abandoned their vehicles after the mountain track had grown too steep, twisting and dangerous.

No amount of sporting activity could replace the cardinal passions of the King for feminine company and for good food. The King's entourage always included a generous number of beautiful women. Ponsonby had a great eye for such detail. At Homburg there were Lord and Lady Cork (he was tiresome, but she amused the King), Lady Boyde and Arthur and Venetia James ('he charming, but not having so much in common with the King except racing; she full of humour and high spirits, walking with the King and keeping him amused'). At Marienbad there were Madame Waddington, Madame de Venay and the 'curious people' the King was in the habit of picking up and inviting back to luncheon, including Madame de Varrue, whose husband had adopted the title Baron without much warrant, and Mrs D. Lace with 'eye-glass, short skirts and a murky past'. It was with great sorrow that the King felt constrained to ban female company at Windsor in 1906 as a token of mourning for the dead King of Denmark, and he lamented 'the tiresome evenings we shall have'. His reputation as Prince of Wales still dogged him – Frederick Ponsonby was confronted in Marienbad by 'a beautiful lady from the half-world of Vienna, who wanted to have the honour of sleeping with the King. On being told this was out of the question, she said if it came to the worst she could sleep with me ... I told her to look elsewhere for a bed!' Those days were gone, but it was still a matter for Ponsonby's delicacy to explain to a noted Copenhagen beauty that the King could not come and visit her because he was visiting one of her rivals instead. Despite his advancing years, Edward was not one to put aside his youthful tastes and in 1905 he parted company with the Queen after a Mediterranean cruise and went on by himself to Paris where he arranged an assignation with a friend, 'who had been a noted beauty', in the Jardin des Plantes. In this case, although the King had ordered total privacy, he was distressed to recognise

'Eye-glass, short skirts and a murky past'

The struggles of the suffragettes in the Edwardian period form a strong contrast to the glamour of fashionable court society. Edward, like his mother, strongly disapproved of the activities of Mrs Pankhurst and her followers, and showed no sympathy with their cause.
LEFT An idealised view of the Women Writer's Suffrage League, 1909.
RIGHT Grim reality: a suffragette leader being carried from Buckingham Palace gates by a policeman.

in the shrubbery the familiar face of one of his detectives who continually protected his safety.

Many of the old Victorian moral barriers were down and the public, in the words of a popular song, could admire:

> The monarch to make things hum,
> The King, the runabout King.

Moreover, as Knollys sensibly pointed out: 'There are some women to whom it is impossible for the Prince to speak for five minutes, without their imagining that he means much more than he thought of.' Ponsonby was perhaps a little prurient: he worried that Maude Walker, who had been invited to dance for the King at Marienbad, had a reputation for performing 'with only two oyster shells and a five franc piece'; in the event, the performance was not indecent, although, as he recorded, 'I cannot say she wore many clothes'. The press was on the whole more cautious about revealing the gossip about the reigning

monarch than they had been about the indiscretions of the Prince of Wales, and it was left to a French politician, Clemenceau, to express the bourgeois distaste for English morals when he told Ponsonby that games of croquet and tennis were but an excuse for young people to make love. The Kaiser was inclined to annoy his uncle by referring to his relationship with Mrs Keppel in disapproving tones, but there was nothing among Edward's friends to compare to the scandal when the Kaiser's close friend, Count Philip Eulenburg, was indicted for homosexual offences in Berlin. Strong feeling in Britain did not arise, as long as the Crown was seen not to be involved in politics nor to make extortionate demands on the Civil List. Of course there were those, like the 'serious' Spencers, who chose not to be drawn into the fashionable circle, but the views of those who were more outspoken were often less attractive than the indiscretions they sought to pillory. 'The King', wrote Lady Paget, 'as King is much more useful than he was as Prince of Wales. He has a great deal of ability but is always surrounded by a bevy of Jews and a ring of racing people. He has the same luxurious tastes as the Semites, the same love of pleasure and comfort.'

In some ways, indeed, the King even appeared on the side of the reformers. He dealt effectively with the drunkenness that had prevailed at Balmoral latterly during Queen Victoria's reign, by dismissing a stalker of thirty years' service, who was found drunk on duty. The frontiers of behaviour had been advanced a long way since his youth, and with some of the trends he was violently out of sympathy – notably in the case of women serving on the Royal Commission on Divorce set up by the Liberal Government, which he called 'the thin edge of suffragetism'. Like many elderly men, he believed that the age of good manners had passed away. At Marienbad once he found out that a Foreign Office official on his staff had kept a lady waiting for a game of golf. 'When I was a young man', Edward declared, 'I was taught never to keep a lady waiting.' On the other hand, Edward was not inclined to try to reverse the decline of the moral imperative, nor to revive the strict code of Victorian ethics. He delighted the moralists by walking out of a somewhat risqué play entitled *Die Hölle (The Underworld)* at Marienbad but his exit was provoked by boredom rather

Sargent's portrait of Lord Ribblesdale seems to epitomise so many of the qualities of the Edwardian aristocrat: the assured, proud leader of society, fond of riding, hunting and shooting – qualities also possessed by Edward himself.

than disgust, and he wrote candidly to the Bishop of Ripon to say that he had 'no wish to pose as a protector of morals, especially abroad'.

A less appealing trait than Edward's love of feminine companionship was the excessive indulgence, even gluttony, which was a marked characteristic of the Edwardian upper class. Edward's love of good food in vast quantities, even as Prince of Wales, had resulted in his naturally portly figure bulging out in a manner reminiscent of his great-uncle, George IV. Shortly before the coronation, the royal waist measured forty-eight inches – the same as his chest. Despite his devotion to correct dress, the King did not look well in the tight uniforms he often wore on his travels in Europe, yet he made no sustained attempt to reduce weight or his gargantuan intake of food. A dinner with Lord Rosebery at Posillipo in 1903 ran to some twenty courses, and the King's own ordinary dinners frequently exceeded twelve. As he got older, he reduced his breakfast to the light Continental model, but if he was going to go shooting that day he always made sure that he was fortified with haddock, poached eggs, bacon, chicken and wood-cock. Luncheon was always a massive indulgence and might include the rich foods of which he was so fond – game stuffed with *foie gras* or truffles, or covered in a heavy sauce. Dinner, however, was the main meal. It was fortunate that, in view of the many formal banquets, the King was able to do justice to the elaborate fancies of his hosts. As late as 1910, just before departing for the last holiday to Biarritz, the King gave a dinner that included turtle soup, salmon steak, grilled chicken, saddle of mutton, snipe with *foie gras*, asparagus, fruit, and an iced delicacy and savouries. Then there were the specialities of the house: deer pie at Balmoral, pigeon pie during Ascot week, and turtle and whitebait for the Derby. Caviar and grilled oysters the King considered perfect appetisers to a really sound meal.

It is understandable that when Esher came to economise on the staff at Buckingham Palace earlier in the reign, he found it impossible to dispense with the services of any of the fifty kitchen staff. The royal chef, Monsieur Ménager, followed the King on all his peregrinations to ensure that the royal palate was not deprived. On top of all this was added a taste for claret (in preference to champagne) and brandy, as well as a capacity for tobacco that would now horrify the Royal College of Surgeons. While he 'limited' himself to one small cigar and a few cigarettes *before* breakfast, Edward smoked on average twelve large cigars and twenty cigarettes a day. Attempts to replace cigars with a pipe or to reduce the amount of tobacco were quite unsuccessful, and it was only on the morning of his death that he failed to enjoy his customary large cigar. No amount of Continental 'cures' could prevent such a regime from taking its toll. In 1904, as they were being guided through the Hamburg Rathaus, Ponsonby noted that the King was 'blowing like a grampus'. In later years, fellow guests noticed his tendency to fall asleep at luncheons, and by 1906 there were distinct signs of bronchial trouble.

Among his more personal attributes, the King cultivated a meticulous interest in questions of fashion and retained in his maturity the taste for clothes which had been a feature of his youth. During his reign he gave the seal of approval to the Norfolk jacket, the Tyrolean hat and the grey felt hat, and he attempted to popularise the style of putting the crease in the trousers on the sides rather than the front. Although unable to prevent the decline of knee-breeches and the frock-coat, the King quashed the fashion for Panama hats in Britain. He was known as one of the most stylish dressers of his day (an exception noted by the *Tailor and Cutter*, however, was the occasion when His Majesty met a friend arriving at Sandringham station, wearing a green cap, pink tie, white gloves, knee-breeches, grey slippers and a brown check overcoat!) and as a stickler for wearing the correct form of dress on each occasion, a form of etiquette whose rules he sometimes laid down. Lord Rosebery was a frequent victim of his quirks: arriving at Buckingham Palace for a formal reception dressed in trousers rather than knee-breeches, Rosebery found himself asked testily 'whether he was in the suite of the American ambassador'. On another occasion the former Prime Minister visited the King at Naples, during the 1907 tour, wearing a white yachting jacket – and compounded the offence by treating it with levity. To Edward such a gaffe was a serious matter. His reprimand was subtle; having asked Rosebery to wait behind until he had finished playing cards, on the expectation of a confidential chat such as Rosebery enjoyed, the King kept the peer waiting for

Edward as the leader of fashion and society. This photograph shows him wearing the Homburg hat, which takes its name from the spa in Germany which he visited as Prince of Wales.

'*He nearly shut
his eyes with
repugnance*'

some time and then simply finished his game and bade him good-night. Rosebery returned, chastened, to Posillipo. Likewise, Sidney Greville was reproved just before leaving for a wedding in the company of the sovereign. 'My dear fellow, ... is it possible you are thinking of going in a black waistcoat?' Frederick Ponsonby, too, incurred the King's displeasure when he appeared in a frock-coat that had once been black but had turned green under the influence of the Mediterranean sun. 'He nearly shut his eyes with repugnance'.

In all matters relating to the granting and wearing of ceremonial orders the King had a serious, even devoted interest. He established the Order of Merit himself, and lavishly distributed the Victorian Order, his own personal gift. He seldom lost an opportunity to tell a person if he was wearing his decorations incorrectly, and picked out at once the mistaken colours of the Garter ribbon on a portrait by the French artist Constant. He was a master of all the grades and precedences of Orders and the subtle distinctions which surrounded their award. It was unthinkable, for example, that a British Order should be given to so minor a prince as Danilo of Montenegro. The King firmly retained this form of patronage in Crown hands, although occasionally he had to yield to the Government over individual cases. He objected to some of the demands of the Liberal Government for the award of the party faithful (not surprisingly, considering the venal origin of many of their qualifications in an age when honours, though not so freely available for cash as in the palmy days of Lloyd George and Maundy Gregory, were still to be had by purchase) and their recommendation of Lord Pirrie, the Belfast industrialist, for the Order of the Knights of St Patrick in 1909, was most uncongenial to him. He was genuinely pleased, however, to give the Garter to his old friend Lord Carrington, and did not hesitate to decorate the Abbot of Tepl, whom he had personally conducted round Windsor, with the KCVO. On occasion, the King could be too generous – his desire to decorate every officer at one naval review caused severe problems for Ponsonby, who had to see to the distribution. It is worth noting that British decorations were very highly sought after on the Continent, and the average distribution of some eight hundred a year was considered parsimonious by European standards.

Keir Hardy by *Spy* in 1906. Keir Hardie first entered Parliament for West Ham, voted in by the dockers. His contempt for fashion, etiquette and social forms set him worlds apart from Edward and his surrounding circle of friends. Keir Hardie stood for social change and Socialism – ideas which Edward was unable to support or accept.

Edward VII was peculiarly aware of the majesty of his position and he made no bones about enjoying it to the full. Like most of his contemporaries he was a snob; he could refer breezily to the Portuguese nobility as resembling 'waiters in a second-class restaurant', and he savoured the atmosphere of the highly exclusive Paris Jockey Club. His own social circle was broad but he rarely sought to break down barriers when he came across them, and he expected all classes to accept him as the social arbiter of his age. When annoyed by the Labour party's opposition in the House of Commons to what they called 'hob-nobbing with blood-stained monsters' (i.e. his visit to the

Czar at Reval in 1908), he immediately cancelled the invitation to Keir Hardie, Victor Grayson and Arthur Ponsonby for a royal garden party given for members of the House of Commons. Keir Hardie characteristically declared that he would never again attend a royal function; but Arthur Ponsonby, brother of the King's assistant private secretary, was pressed to make a full apology to the King for his language before he could be readmitted to court favour. Evidently the King felt it necessary to administer a social rebuff, although this involved him in the charge of interfering in a House of Commons debate. On most occasions, though, the King's sense of delicacy was an asset and the household could take pride in it on all state occasions. Comparing the urbane confidence of the sovereign and his Queen with the inept performance of the French President and his wife at a reception in 1907, Ponsonby told a French courtier, 'What can you expect? Yours are amateurs and ours are professionals at this game.' The French must have been thrilled.

Given that the greater part of the King's encounters with the outside world were formal, Edward possessed most, if not all, of the regal attributes. He was a good listener and once sustained a description of the workings of a submarine twice in a short space of time, without showing any signs of impatience. He had the knack of saying the right thing when it was required – F. E. Smith (later Lord Birkenhead) was most impressed early in his career as a Conservative MP, when the King told him that he always read his speeches. (It may have been true: Smith was the most lively speaker of the day.) The King's diplomatic ability was founded on experience, but also on supreme self-confidence. Those who watched, spoke of his 'sixth sense' in dealing with people. When a visiting Indian prince was seen at Buckingham Palace to be throwing the stalks of his asparagus on the floor, the King calmly followed suit. Even when he was bored, he was tactful in extracting himself, and when stuck at the Longchamps races with Madame Loubet and the wife of the Governor of Paris in 1903, he went to some trouble to manufacture an invitation to the former to come and inspect the new stand of the Jockey Club – alone. His treatment of servants also won him credit; not every king in Europe followed his invariable habit of saying 'thank-you' when they had rend-

'Yours are amateurs and ours are professionals at this game'

ered him a service. True, he could be unfairly angry – a lady who had the misfortune to fall over at a court reception, found her name removed from the court lists forthwith – but rudeness was far from his character. He could be blunt with those whom he knew well. He once told the Duchess of Rutland, 'You don't brush your hair'. But when the Duke of Fife found his name omitted from the list of guests at Windsor Castle after Queen Victoria's funeral and Edward reproved the man responsible in the Duke's presence, he called him back after Fife had left and apologised: 'I know how difficult it has been for you ... I had to say something as Fife was so hurt.' There was no meanness in his nature and it well became the ruler of the greatest Empire that, in the words of Sir Edward Grey, 'He had a capacity for enjoying life ... combined with a positive and strong desire that everyone else should enjoy life too.'

The essence of the King's popularity is harder to define. His colourful character obviously appealed to the mass readership of what G. M. Young called the 'flash' post-Victorian era; but that generation was also more conscious than the preceding one of status and formal prestige. The Edwardian decade was marked in many ways by uneasy questioning of the position and future of Britain, no longer indisputably the richest and most powerful country in the world, and there was a great deal to be said for having at the top a head of State fully conscious of the value of pomp and drama in political life. Certainly there is something charismatic in the reaction of the populace to him: large crowds gathered at every public appearance, and pieces of furniture from his rooms in the Hotel Weimar at Marienbad were sold for double their value after the King's departure each year. In 1910, while visiting the Sassoons in Brighton, Edward went to sleep in his car on Worthing seafront and woke up to find his vehicle surrounded by a loyal but almost impassable crowd. The monarchy itself may no longer have been a real force in politics but it had acquired new dimensions as a symbolic institution. At times Edward found the attention paid to him rather unwelcome. 'The King's one idea of happiness', Ponsonby wrote, 'was to be in the middle of a crowd with no one taking any notice of him.' Hence he would resort to the expedient of travelling under an alias, usually that of Duke of Lancaster. But this, too, could present difficulties; on one occasion the King found it difficult to gain access to the ex-Empress Eugénie because her servants did not recognise him as King of England. In any case, the chosen alias soon became public and the portly 'Professor Lankaster' found an undue amount of attention waiting for him when he arrived at Marienbad.

In Britain, Edward began to bridge the gap between the withdrawn eminence of Queen Victoria and the more open style increasingly developed by his son, George V, and grand-sons, Edward VIII and George VI. He ignored the danger of over-exposure implicit in Ponsonby's warnings to Haakon VII of Norway not to diminish the royal ethos: 'They [the people] were bound to be disappointed if they saw him going about like an ordinary man in the street.' Edward's frequent journeys about the country enabled many towns and thousands of people to see the sovereign for the first time in half a century. In some areas it had been far longer: Edward was the first king to visit the Isle of Man since Canute. Even in rebellious Ireland 'the attitude of the people in the streets ... seemed most loyal – but dissociated the King and Queen entirely from the Government'.

The King was involved in valuable social work, notably in the field of medical provision. The Hospital Fund in which he had been involved since 1897 continued, under the name of King Edward's Hospital Fund, and donations grew from £50,000 to £153,000 a year during his reign. He helped to found Midhurst Sanatorium for tuberculosis cases (in his own words, 'a sanatorium for the poorer middle classes') and after he had had a face ulcer removed by radium he displayed a deep interest in the development of the substance in medicine. Nor was there any let-up in the round of formal ceremonies – opening buildings, docks and bridges, which required tireless reserves of energy and tact.

Nevertheless a huge gulf yawned between the life of the King and that of the mass of his subjects. A private visit to the slums of Naples in 1903 and the experience of the Housing Commission in 1884 moved him emotionally, without enlarging in any practical sense his social conscience. In preparation for the Lords' debate on working-class housing, in February 1884,

Edward paid a visit to the Clerkenwell slums in disguise, accompanied by Lord Carrington and a police escort. Horrified by the degradation that he witnessed he made to empty his pockets of gold sovereigns; but the gesture was restrained by the others, who feared a riot. His attitude to social change remained that of Burke rather than Keir Hardie and he accepted as a fact of life the inevitability of the *status quo*. He passed through many industrial towns but went on always to the country houses beyond, where he stayed whilst attending functions and ceremonies. Although in 1897 Sidney Webb had assured him of the loyalty of British Socialists to the Crown, Edward himself never really trusted the radicals. Even the appointment of the staid John Burns to the Local Government Board in 1905 led to rumblings about the 'republican' reputation of the first working-class MP to become a minister. Burns soon passed into royal favour, perhaps because of his moderation, or perhaps because of his good clothes sense. In Margot Tenant's words, 'Just as the Lord Mayor represented commerce, the Prime Minister the Government, and the Commons the people, the King represented Society'. Society meant the rich – the plutocratic trends rather than the egalitarian. Although the King had come into contact with many types of individual, Ponsonby wondered after the Irish visit of 1907, whether in the wider context, 'this was much use as far as the people were concerned'. Recipients of the many gold and silver cigarette-cases, some of which were monogrammed with the King's cipher in diamonds, were not usually on the bread-line themselves. There was no effort on the King's part to choose his companions in order to give himself a deeper understanding of the nation over which he reigned; and the outsiders were, more often than not, interesting eccentrics, drawn from his own class, such as the French pacifist Baron d'Estournelles or the Prince of Monaco, a deep-sea fishing enthusiast, who went with the King on his visit to Kiel in 1904. King Edward's style of life was indeed that of the image of splendid and easy living, to which the survivors of the holocaust of World War I looked back as to a vanished paradise; but it was totally out of touch with the forces of discontent and anxiety building up in British society – which were to plunge the country into the period of *Sturm und Drang* after 1910.

'*The King represented Society*'

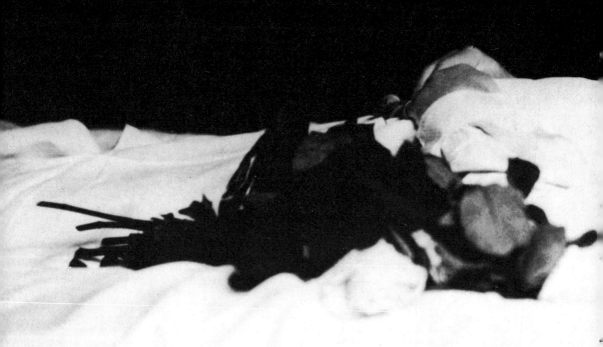

8 The Passing of

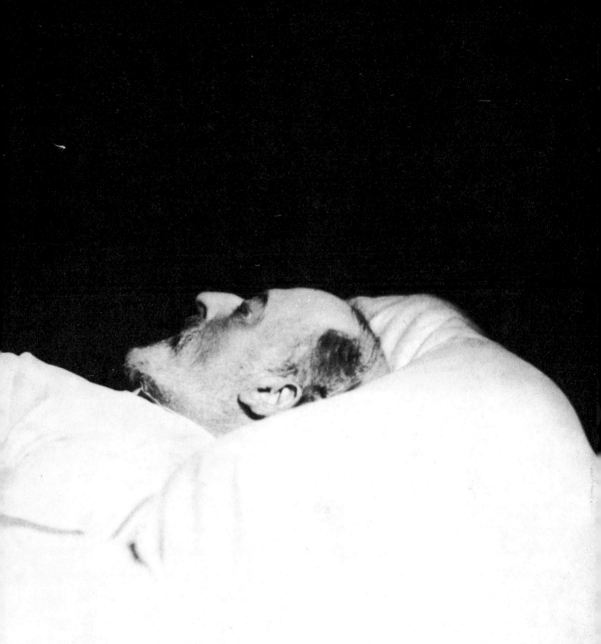

an Era 1910

One of the last photographs taken of Edward.

PREVIOUS PAGES
Edward lying in state in Westminster Hall, May 1910.

Aᴛᴛᴇʀ 1906 the King's health began slowly to decline. He suffered a series of minor injuries – the accident to his knee-cap aboard Sir Thomas Lipton's yacht, and other leg injuries as a result of tripping in a rabbit hole in Windsor Park in 1905 – but the chief trouble was an increasing number of bronchial attacks. In 1909, during his State visit to Berlin, he collapsed whilst in conversation with Princess Daisy of Pless, whose immediate thought was 'My God, he is dying! Oh, why not in his own country!' This paroxysm passed, but the royal physicians were increasingly concerned about his health. When Edward visited Biarritz for the last time in 1910, the cure, as always, made him feel better but the relief soon passed after his return to London at the end of April. On 30 April, feeling a little unwell, he insisted on spending a cold and rainy afternoon inspecting the planting of crops. When he returned to Buckingham Palace on 2 May, a severe bronchial attack took place. Insisting on completing business as usual, he met the American ambassador, who noticed how ill he looked: 'It seems to me that these attacks are coming on more frequently within the last two years'.

By 4 May even the King recognised how weak he was, but he told one of the permanent heads of the Civil Service: 'I shall not give in – I shall work to the end. Of what use is it to be alive if one cannot work?' The next day he gave his last audience to an official visitor, the Agent-General for Queensland. The Queen had returned hastily from Corfu to find that, for once, the King was unable to meet her at the station. As the whole royal family assembled on 5 May, Edward himself remained in good spirits, asserting that he was 'feeling better and intend to fight this. I shall be about again in a day'. His doctors were far more worried and that evening issued a bulletin announcing that the sovereign was suffering from bronchitis and that 'his condition causes some anxiety'. There was little public alarm as yet. The King insisted on formal dress when he got up and met Sir Ernest Cassel during the morning. His friend left, however, suspecting that the visit might have been his last. Frederick Ponsonby saw the King before handing over his duty, which he shared on a rota with Arthur Davidson, and although he brought a few documents for signature, he felt constrained to keep back Foreign Office despatches 'that would have necessitated a discussion and therefore conversation'. At the end, Edward said goodbye to him 'in case I don't see you again'. On the afternoon of 6 May, the King collapsed and was carried to an armchair. A series of heart attacks followed. His closest friends, including Alice Keppel, were called in to take their farewells. They were ushered into the room where Edward sat hunched up, cheerful to the last, but with an ashen pallor. Already he could hardly breathe. Despite his repeated assertion that he 'would fight it', he was moved into his bed and the doctors, who had by now abandoned hope, gave morphia to relieve the pain. Just before he fell into the final coma, he declared: 'No I shall not give in; I shall go on; I shall work to the last.' The Archbishop of Canterbury had waited in an adjoining room and shortly after 11.45 p.m. he uttered a short prayer as Edward quietly died.

The crowd waiting outside the Palace heard the news at midnight and the effect on the nation was all the more crushing because it had been unexpected. To pay their respects to the dead King, a quarter of a million people filed past the coffin lying in state in Westminster Hall, and huge crowds lined the route of the funeral cortège through London on 20 May. Once again, the crowned heads of Europe made their way to London to attend the funeral, among them the Kaiser, the Kings of Belgium, Bulgaria, Denmark, Greece, Norway, Portugal and Spain, the Archduke Franz Ferdinand of Austria-Hungary and the Dowager Empress of Russia. All the leaders of British politics attended. Asquith had eloquently recorded his thoughts as his ship sailed through the Bay of Biscay on its way home:

'The sense of personal loss ... is extraordinary'

> I went up on deck and the first sight that met my eyes in the twilight before dawn was Halley's comet blazing in the sky ... I felt bewildered and stunned ... we had lost, without warning or preparation, the Sovereign whose ripe experience, trained sagacity, equitable judgement and unvarying consideration counted for so much. For two years I had been his Chief Minister ... [his] unbroken confidence lightened the load which I should otherwise have found almost intolerably oppressive.

Lord Morley, Secretary of State for India, wrote to the Viceroy:

> the feeling of grief and the sense of personal loss throughout the country, indeed throughout Western Europe is extraordinary. It is in a way deeper and keener than when Queen Victoria died ... more

personal. He had just the character that Englishmen, at any rate, thoroughly understand, thoroughly like …. He combined regal dignity with *bonhomie*, and strict regard for form with entire absence of spurious pomp.

Even the Irish press paid tribute to Edward's ability as a peace-maker; and Sir Edward Grey, with his gift for melancholy epigraphs, wrote later: 'He became intensely and increasingly popular and when he died the unprecedently long-drawn-out procession to pass the bier of State in Westminster Hall was a manifestation of genuine and personal sorrow as well as national mourning.'

'*I am heart-broken and overwhelmed with grief*'

Nowhere was grief more profoundly felt than among the royal family. In his diary, Prince George put simply: 'I have lost the best friend and the best of fathers. I never had a cross word with him in my life. I am heart-broken and overwhelmed with grief.' Queen Alexandra brought herself to confide in Ponsonby: 'she had been turned into stone, unable to cry, unable to grasp the meaning of it all, and incapable of doing anything … she would like to go and hide in the country'. Whatever lapses there had been on Edward's part, the family had been sustained by love, affection and mutual respect. Prince George had stepped into the gap left by the death of the unhappy Duke of Clarence and the King had given him his complete trust. Edward did not impose the strict regime which he had suffered himself, and he was prepared to respect the sensitive nature of his heir. Such a pattern was unique in the annals of the Hanoverian dynasty: the curse of the eighteenth century had been finally laid to rest. By his grandchildren too, Edward was much loved. They were encouraged to call him 'Kingy' in private and with them he abandoned the public face. 'Good morning, children, am I not a funny looking old man?' he cried, when he found them over-awed by the coronation ceremony. A fundamental belief in the value of the family was the Victorian virtue which Edward found most easy and natural to accept.

The King's death left his successor with a constitutional crisis on his hands, as the Liberal Government debated whether to demand a royal guarantee to create enough peers to ensure the passage of the Parliament Bill. But in the aftermath of national mourning, an attempt was made to bring about an agreement

Edward and Alexandra
on the royal yacht at
Cowes, 1909.

between the Liberals and the Conservatives, through a conference of leaders. When this broke down on 10 November,
King George found himself faced with the same intractable
problem that had agonised his father; only, as Asquith reflected,
he lacked his father's experience of the world. Consequently,
the battle over whether the King should give Asquith a
guarantee was fought out among the private secretaries. After a
good deal of intrigue, Knollys succeeded in influencing the
King to accept the necessity of giving Asquith his promise.
With this secured, and a Liberal-Labour-Irish Nationalist
majority returned at the second general election of 1910, the

213

way was open to force the Parliament Bill through the Lords. The political crisis exploded. In a famous scene in the House of Commons on 24 June 1911, Asquith was howled down by a group of recalcitrant Tories who did not scruple to raise the damning cry 'Who killed the King?' Queen Alexandra hinted, according to Ponsonby, that the political crisis of 1910 might have hastened the King's illness; and William II wrote to Bethman-Hollweg that 'the P.M. and other of his colleagues were publicly hissed in the streets, and expressions like "You have killed the King" were heard'. The 'Truce of God', declared after Edward's death, postponed but could not prevent the bitterness of the climax of political conflict in the overheated summer of 1911.

During the passage of the Parliament Bill, the politicians treated King George's position with respect, but they did not attempt to hide the fact that, for the monarchy, an era had ended. 'The greatest of our Kings since William the Conqueror' – Harcourt's verdict on the late sovereign – may have been hyperbole exaggerated by hindsight, yet Edward was perhaps the last ruler who was a public personality in his own right. His successor, better schooled in the conventions and responsibilities of a constitutional monarch, more in tune with the democratic age, and often shrewder in the political questions of the day, even so lacked the forcefulness and flair of Edward's style. Only with Edward dead, could Asquith advance the proposition: 'It is not the function of a constitutional sovereign to act as arbiter or mediator between rival parties and policies.' Whereas Queen Victoria had always seen herself above politics and King Edward had always insisted on his right to consultation, King George had to reconcile himself to accepting dictation if his opinions clashed with those of his minister.

But it was in more than a constitutional sense that Edward's death signified an end of an era. 'I always felt', Victoria Sackville-West wrote, 'he kept things together somehow.' In his own person Edward was a link between the security and stability of the mid-nineteenth century and the uncertain passages of the twentieth. Just as later commentators looked back to the Edwardian era as a haven of peace before the tempest of the 1914 War, so his contemporaries saw in the King a living monument to a generation untroubled by doubts about

Britain's economic predominance and strategic safety. The King's death divides the period 1900–14; it was during the last four years that the country was beset by the troubles chronicled in George Dangerfield's mordant book *The Strange Death of Liberal England.* Syndicalism, doctrines of class warfare, militant suffragettism, threats of Ulster rebellion, swelled into a menace so great that it obscured the onset of the European war. The death of Edward was not, of course, in any real sense a cause of the discontents, but it became a symbolic marker to those who looked back. He was more than a figurehead, and his removal opened up the unease of many people at the latent violence of a society growing increasingly complex and estranged from traditional reassurance. Dangerfield summed up the King's appeal in psychological terms – 'he represented in a concentrated shape, those bourgeois kings whose florid forms and rather dubious escapades were all the industrialised world had left of an ancient divinity; his people saw in him the personification of something nameless, genial and phallic'. His successor was merely dull and 'dullness was almost unforgivable in 1910'. The excitement which Edward had brought, the re-enactment of a splendid drama, gave harmless and vicarious pleasure. The demands which followed were not to be satisfied so easily.

His political and diplomatic acumen was celebrated by the biographers, some of whom, in retrospect, tended to regard him as the moulder of his times and not merely its symbol. Edward Legge (who wrote two books to prove his point, *King Edward in his True Colours* [1912] and *More About King Edward* [1913]) thought the lengthy account of him given by Sir Sydney Lee in the Dictionary of National Biography insufficiently laudatory in tone. In the introduction to that volume of DNB, Lee wrote of his attempts,

> made, it is believed for the first time, to coordinate the manifold activities of the sovereign in a just historic and biographic spirit .... The prominent place which the late King filled for half a century in the nation's public life, both before and after his accession, seemed, in the absence of a full record elsewhere, to compel a treatment which should be as exhaustive and authoritative as the writer's knowledge allowed.

Later editions have been less effusive; see, for example, the space allotted to George VI in the most recent volumes. Yet it was Lee

'I always felt he kept things together somehow'

Funeral of Edward VII, May 1910.
The front line of mourners are,
left to right, the Kaiser William II,
George V, the Duke of Connaught.
They are followed by
the Prince of Wales (now
Duke of Windsor) and Prince Albert
(later George VI).

who was chosen to write the official biography; in which he presented the picture of a forceful character, seeking independence and the rights of personal initiative but hemmed in, both by the restrictions of constitutional reality and his own nature. Others denigrated his achievements: Dangerfield condemned him as a misguided royal fop, and even the judicious Halévy suggested that 'In him the monarchy was honoured rather than the monarch. It would certainly not be very long [after his death] before it was perceived how superficial his popularity had been.'

In comparison with other European monarchs, however, Edward was neither subtle genius, éminence grise, nor hedonistic fool. Brought up and choosing to live within the restricted élite, accepting the conventions of the society he himself found most attractive, he arouses in the modern observer feelings of both envy and sympathy – envy for the elegant, leisured ideal of existence, sympathy for the stifling restrictions on thought and action which his status involved. Representing society, he in fact lived totally outside it, nor did he ever understand the forces of change that worked in a democratic age. Believing that he occupied a position of power and responsibility, he received the respect of those who did control power – but he reigned at a time when the royal province had diminished. In such conditions it was left to his successor, more insular, cautious and realistic, if no less conservative and patriotic, to preserve the symbolic authority of the Crown.

Bibliography

BIOGRAPHIES

Sir S. Lee, *King Edward VII, A Biography*, 2 vols, 1925–27
Sir Philip Magnus, *King Edward VII*, 1964
V. Cowles, *Edward VII and His Circle*, 1956
G. Dangerfield, *Victoria's Heir*, 1942
E. F. Benson, *King Edward VII*, 1933
H. E. Wortham, *King Edward VII*, 1933
S. Munz, *King Edward VII at Marienbad*, 1934
Sir S. Lee (ed.), *Dictionary of National Biography*, 2nd supplement, 1912
A. Maurois, *Edward VII and His Times*, 1933
Sir H. Nicolson, *George V*, 1952

GENERAL ACCOUNTS

S. Nowell-Smith (ed.), *Edwardian England* (especially R. Fulford,
   'The Monarchy'), 1964
B. Tuchman, *The Proud Tower*, 1966
V. Sackville-West, *The Edwardians*, 1935
P. Hearnshaw (ed.), *Edwardian England*, 1933
J. B. Priestley, *The Edwardians*, 1970
J. P. Mackintosh, *The British Cabinet*, 2nd edition, 1968
E. Halévy, *History of the English People in the Nineteenth Century*,
   (especially volumes v and vi), paperback, 1961
G. M. Young, *Victorian England, Portrait of an Age*, 1936

MEMOIRS AND RECOLLECTIONS OF CONTEMPORARIES

Sir F. Ponsonby (Lord Syonby), *Recollections of Three Reigns*, 1951
Lord Esher, *The Influence of King Edward*, 1915
Sir John Fisher, *Memories*, 1919
G. Cornwallis-West, *Edwardian Hey-Days*, 1930
L. Langtry, *The Days I knew*, 1925
A. G. Gardiner, *Prophets, Priests and Kings*, 1908
C. Sykes, *Four Studies in Loyalty*, 1946
Sir L. Jones, *An Edwardian Youth*, 1956
H. J. Bruce, *Silken Dalliance*, 1946
A. Wingate, *That Mighty City*, 1913
Letters of Queen Victoria, 1907, 1926–8, 1930–2

Index